ALONG THE WACCAMAW

ALONG THE WACCAMAW

by Randall A. Wells

with Illustrations by Robert Alden Rubin

ALGONQUIN BOOKS OF CHAPEL HILL

1990

Published by Algonquin Books of Chapel Hill
Post Office Box 2225
Chapel Hill, North Carolina 27515-2225
a division of Workman Publishing Company, Inc.
708 Broadway
New York, New York 10003

Illustration of Glen Ellyn Station, page 35, based on
materials provided by Lee Hesterman.

Library of Congress Cataloging-in-Publication Data
Wells, Randall A., 1942–
Along the Waccamaw / by Randall A. Wells.
p.   cm. —(American places of the heart)
ISBN 0-912697-93-8
1. Wells, Randall A., 1942–   .   2. Conway (S.C.)—Biography.
3. Conway (S.C.)—Social life and customs.   4. Glen Ellyn (Ill.)—
Biography.   I. Title.   II. Series.
F279.C75W45   1990
975.7'87—dc20   89-27426 CIP

1   3   5   7   9   10   8   6   4   2

First Edition

To Tom Hollinger

Contents

CONTENTS

Acknowledgments

I thank my wife, Marjory Wells, for her summer "grants," as well as for her advice, encouragement, patience, and eventually just tolerance. She said it best: "When this book is over, I think you should get me the biggest diamond you can find!"

To Andrea and Katie, I apologize for the time lavished on symbols instead of daughters. But I hope that someday you will have an experience as gratifying as this work has been to me.

My gratitude goes to Mr. Jim Cato, former editor of the Conway (S.C.) *Field & Herald*, for agreeing to print a series of columns titled "Mr. Newcomb" that formed the kernel of *Along the Waccamaw*.

Once again I thank the people who read one version or another of the manuscript and offered suggestions: Ms. Christa Hunter, Mr. Warren Miller, Mrs. Catherine H. Lewis, Mr. George W. Carleton, Prof. S. Paul Rice, Prof. Susan Webb, Rev. J. Gregory Prior, Prof. Joseph N. Pinson, Mrs. Elizabeth W. Shaw, and Prof. Charles W. Joyner.

I am grateful to Mrs. Delia Groom for her kind gift of money, which enabled me to buy a computer during the last stage of writing. For much typing in earlier stages I thank Ms. Shirell J. Mishoe, School of Humanities and Fine Arts, Coastal Carolina College of the University of South Carolina.

Also I am grateful to both Coastal Carolina College and the Horry County Higher Educational Commission for the subvention grant toward publication. For working with the Commission, I also thank Dr. Ronald G. Eaglin, Chancellor of Coastal Carolina College, Dr. James Rex, former Vice-Chancellor for Academic Affairs, and Col. William Baxley, Associate Chancellor for College Advancement.

My appreciation goes to Ms. Marjorie Hudson, copyeditor, for her sharp eyes and tactful words.

And to Mr. Louis Rubin, Jr., editor of Algonquin Books of Chapel Hill, I acknowledge a great debt. He saw promise in the manuscript and, by a sort of correspondence course, helped me to bring it out.

Randall A. Wells
Conway, South Carolina

ALONG THE WACCAMAW

1

The Waccamaw River

The water, glittering and dark, flowed past our cottage toward the Intracoastal Waterway, Winyah Bay, and the Atlantic Ocean. Marco Polo might have returned with the tale of such a river to match his report of black rocks that burned. The Waccamaw (pronounced Walk-a-maw) carried patches of wet sky and of shimmering clouds, and now in autumn it also doubled the yellow and rust-red tops of cypress trees on the opposite bank, even inundating their upright knees during a flood that reached the first stair of our porch. To Marge, this abundance of trees contrasted with the cracked, barren banks of the Pecos River in her hometown of Carlsbad, New Mexico. Under their overhanging branches and in channels hidden alongside them sat fishermen with little electric motors and patient stratagems; on weekends the wakes from motorboats lapped their trunks while on the open river many a skier gripped the taut rope and slapped across those wakes.

Somebody told me the darkness of the water was caused by cypress knees, but I was unsure. Pollution? Not a sign. Somebody also said that the river rose and fell with the tides, but I never did notice any such rhythm.

"Can you swim in it?" we had wondered at first. Less prudent than I, Marge lowered herself from the dock.

"What's it like?"

"Clean . . . cold . . . very black . . . and scary." Her dip over, she reported that she had feared snakes, yet couldn't see down into the water. "I felt like I was plunging off into the unknown."

Our landlord had given us permission to use an old rowboat lying on the bank. Since its oarlocks were broken, we found canoe paddles and hauled it into the water to go exploring a few times. Once, in high spirits, I stood up to pole the boat up a creek, as we had done in the bayous when Marge was in nurse-midwifery school. It wasn't long before a loud splash drew raucous laughter.

I tried fishing a couple of times with the bobber that Beth, Marge's friend from school, gave me as a going-away present. "Just tie it to your big toe," she directed in her New Orleans accent, "and fish from your back pawch." She had to correct me when I kept calling it a "bobbin," the closest word in my vocabulary and one that I had heard when my mother sewed on Great Grandmother Capps's machine. I had fished only once in my suburban hometown, when my father and I—the family still without a car after World War II—hiked two and a half miles to the forest preserve. Now, from the Waccamaw, the only thing I ever caught was the end of the pole itself, which flew off during a cast and stayed in the drink by virtue of a stuck hook. Luckily my dad was visiting at Christmas and worked a grapple from the rowboat while I fought the current and my mother, onshore, fought laughter.

One day Marge and I glided and paddled downstream in stillness, no engine to distract us, no easy speed to detach us. Owing to our defective teamwork, however, we made numerous unnecessary tacks and rode broadside now and then, so the banks sometimes echoed our mirth as well as the thunk of paddle against wood.

After passing the last house, then rounding curve after unfamiliar curve, we finally decided to head back. But set against our return was not only the current but the wind. We now had to paddle hard just to stay in place, and strain to make each foot of headway. With muscles and faces tightened, we pulled and grunted, while the wind stirred up little wavelets before it rushed into our eyes. Bush by bush we fought our way upstream. Halfway back we struggled into a little cove to secure the boat against a low branch and rest. Under way again, at last we spotted the lovely dark green of our cottage, and soon we were collapsing into bed.

One night my sleep was disturbed by the noise of an engine. Never had I heard such a sound at night, for boaters always scurried to put in before dark. As it grew louder I sensed the difference: not the usual buzzsaw sound but a low pumping that suggested a reserve of power. I lay awake while it progressed upstream with an imposing steadiness. Maybe a large houseboat, I conjectured. What kind of light must it have to be able to search out the channel and spot any debris? As the sound drew further away in the night, I grew sleepier, and the next day I wondered if it had even existed.

Within a week that deep murmur came to me again in the daytime. Hurrying into the bedroom I flung open the curtain. There was a ship in my backyard. For a moment I could see no water, just vessel. Its prow was curved and the surface of its hull nothing but rust; its long deck held neither superstructure nor cargo, but instead, tall snakelike objects that jutted up every few yards, rusted pipes or burned tree trunks. Behind this apparition I felt somewhat relieved to see a tugboat. When its stern finally came into view, I read the nameplate aloud in wonder: *Samson II-Charleston.*

～～～

Beth had helped Marge drive her Mustang from Vicksburg, and now we were seeing her off at the Conway bus station. Through the dusk I noticed a big wooden object lying in the vacant lot across from us. I made out two sides that tapered to a point at one end and at the other widened to form a sort of box, while the top bowed upward somewhat: an upside-down rowboat.

Pretty tacky, I thought. Many a bus traveler would remember Conway from that scene. A few weeks later the object was gone — but by then I had got to know the community better, and I wondered if something of significance had not been carried off with the boat. Scraped and painted, it would have made a fitting emblem for the town.

For the Waccamaw River defined not only the city's limits but its heritage. Flowing from a spring-fed lake in North Carolina, the Waccamaw had helped to isolate the area until comparatively recent days. For centuries it had served as the main highway.

Horry County, pronounced "O'Ree," was South Carolina's largest. It was shaped somewhat like a diamond that had been deeply eroded on two sides. These northwestern and southwestern sides were formed by rivers, the Little Pee Dee and (to the far north) the Lumber. Its northeastern side was a straight line made by the North Carolina–South Carolina border. Its southeastern side was the gently concave shoreline of the Atlantic Ocean that formed Long Bay.

From Conway, a twelve-mile drive east along Route 378 led to the Little Pee Dee. A twenty-seven-mile drive west on Highway 90 led to the diamond's northeastern corner, where

6

North and South Carolina met the ocean. A thirteen-mile drive to the southeast reached to the end of Highway 501 in Myrtle Beach. Almost thirty miles of Horry County extended above Conway, and seventeen below it.

The Waccamaw, forming the town's eastern border, split the county itself into two parts as it flowed roughly to the southwest, parallel to the Atlantic. A further schism was made by the Intracoastal Waterway, which also ran along the coast, a mile or so inland, and passed beneath only three bridges in thirty miles.

Water and swamps had helped to isolate the area since the time of the first Indian footprint. Although the first train had arived from North Carolina in 1887, not until 1902 had a primitive highway bridge been erected across the Little Pee Dee at Galivants Ferry; in 1904 Conway had become connected on the north by a drawbridge, and on the east by a turntable bridge across the Waccamaw just before World War I. Marge and I were trying to put down roots into a boggy area of South Carolina that its proud citizens—having lived mainly off its water and land for almost two hundred and fifty years—proudly called the Independent Republic of Horry.

Many natives even bore a mark to identify them: a brown stain on the teeth. But if cigarette smoking was the reason, surely children did not have the habit? I soon learned that the cause was what else but the local water, which contained excessive natural fluoride.

The language of the natives, in its isolation, had remained a different species. Words like "this" and "that" were pronounced "dis" and "dat"; a "building" was a "beeowding"; "when" was always "whenever," and "whenever" was "everwhen"; "again" was sometimes "agayne"; the "t" in "auto" was doubled to "aut-toe." For "fire" I expected "fahr" but often heard "fye-yer" (ditto "tye-yer"). Speakers made liberal use of the glottal stop, a consonant formed by closing the throat to stop the airstream (as in the Brooklyn pronunciation of "bottle"). So "doctor" was often "do'ter." I was intrigued to hear the Independent Republic's very own words for the interjection "ouch" or "ow": "OH-wee" or "OW-wee."

That old wooden boat had doubtless made trips without number across that dark element of isolation and transportation, up and down it, and into the swamps, first with oars attached, then an engine. What longtime Conway family was without a memory of such a vessel? How many families who now planed along the river in fiberglass used to putt-putt in metal or row in wood? And how many recreational fishermen had ancestors who used to drop a hook for grub? Fish—one of the Five F's of Conway's heritage, the others being Forest, Field, Family, and Faith. Indeed, the whole rural heritage of the town was expressed by this plain and durable boat.

Not that pedestrians had to dodge jets of chewed tobacco in Conway. But despite many changes over the years, the place retained a definite country twang. People really did say "young'uns," and a woman who sold us curtain material said "hit" for "it." Conway was a side-door, carport, and first-name town. ("I'm Randall Wells." "Hello, Randy.") My brother commented on how friendly people were: "The other drivers wave at you."

Many of its ten thousand residents had been raised on farms. One woman had a house in town and one at the beach, but wanted to move back to the sticks some day, declaring, "I'm a country girl." A fair number of town citizens still operated farms, often with the help of tenants. "In the old days," one member of the Lions Club told me, "the only way to get by was to hold down a job and farm on the side."

Many who worked in the town lived in the country, sometimes in little communities like Ketchuptown that only natives could find. And many rural people came to town to shop, visit the doctor, and run errands, sometimes in bare feet. "I weren't sure which'n was the noodle soup," said an illiterate farmer whom I assisted in the grocery store. A few businesses offered credit until the crop was cashed in.

Where my own hometown was influenced in so many ways by the nearby city of Chicago, Conway was influenced by the surrounding countryside. One of my students at the college wrote about his first disastrous attempts to plow behind a horse. Bumper stickers read "I'm proud to be a farmer," and "Designate Horry Warehouse." A surprising number of residents had "worked 'bacca," a hot, dirty, and tedious job with its "topping" and "suckering." "Never again!" vowed one veteran who had dashed his last hornworm to the ground. On the radio I once heard a rhapsodic guitar that promised a love song but introduced the question, "If you lost money from nematodes and fungus in your tobacco last year . . ." In another commercial, Johnny Cash himself praised a local grocery store by strumming hard on a "folks like you" theme.

"Folks"—that oilcloth-and-overalls word jarred against my background. I said "my parents," not "the folks," and never "Momma 'n Daddy." I could not call a minister a "preacher" because it stripped him of his divinity degree, replaced his library with the Good Book, and shrunk or lengthened his coatsleeves a few too many inches.

When meeting someone for the first time, I would often hear, "What church do you go to?" ("None," I once replied ungraciously.) The mechanic who took care of the Mustang had a Bible on his cigarette machine. And church meant Protestant: only 2 percent of South Carolinians were Roman Catholic. "Do Catholics go to church on *Sunday?*" asked one native. Although St. James Church did exist, it shared its priest with another, and most of its communicants were imports like Marge. There was no Lutheran Church, in contrast to the two in my hometown. And the tiny Episcopal building indicated that in the days of slavery the upperclass English plantation owners had never reached Horry County and its hardscrabble farmers.

For all this religion, citizens paid scant attention to a date that still cast a shadow on my calendar.

"Do you think we should have Lions Club on Good Friday?" I asked a fellow member.

"Why not?" he replied with some heat. Abashed, I felt it useless to describe that long, somber Friday afternoon service when the black-clad ministers of my hometown in Illinois conducted the funeral of Jesus.

College sports were a second religion. Clemson University, formerly an agricultural college, was located on the opposite side of the state, but apparently enjoyed the loyalty of every second person in town. A subdivision near Conway included both a Clemson Road and a Clemson Drive. But to me the school's absorption with spectator sports hinted at the town's cultural thinness and homogeneity.

Just as superficial were the beauty contests, and just as old-fashioned in the way they polarized male and female. Every institution had its vestal. Even tots had their Miss Baby Bikini or Pampers Princess contests (or whatever they called them).

I craved the sound of classical music for its heightening and enriching order. But no such records could be bought locally. The town did, however, boast its own country music station and fireworks store. My sense of isolation deepened when I plugged in the TV and got "snow."

When I had lived in Laramie, Wyoming, for the first few

days at 7,200 feet above sea level I could not quite get enough oxygen. Now, at 120 feet, I was also gasping, figuratively anyway.

~~~

If the Southerner tended to be a homebody more than other Americans, a person from this area out-Dixied Dixie in the inclination to "take my stand, to live and die" there. Natives tended to stay, or, if leaving, to return. When I asked one child how much his friends traveled, he answered, "Maybe to Grandmother's house, that's all." I learned, however, that many families owned beach houses, so there was less reason to travel farther than the ocean. The Grand Strand, a wide beach and booming resort, stretched along the coast for forty-five miles.

Interest in family history? According to a Lions Club joke, Southerners, like Chinamen, eat rice and worship their ancestors. Looking back to the town I had known as home, by contrast, I remembered little such interest. That Tom Hollinger's father had helped build the family's old house presented a fascinating detail without a context. My mother had grown up in the town and had attended the same schools I had, even under the same principals. And certainly it was curious that my grandfather Capps had owned a dry goods store downtown, but I was never sure where. From Conway, I wondered if people in my town had undervalued such historical ties.

~~~

My ambivalence about this new place even extended to the river. It was the source, someone explained, of our telephone problem. The local cooperative, a vestige of yesteryear, could barely connect to a different outfit on the town side of the

Waccamaw. We even had to call long distance to get Conway information. All this was a throwback to the ferry-crossing days, and was especially irksome to one raised in a stronghold of the Bell System.

We would dial 248-2956, for example, yet reach 365-2956, somewhere else in the cooperative's purview; then try again only to reach another number; then have to ask the operator for help. The system had spells. One afternoon I dialed 248-9188 five times and after a few initial clicks never heard a sound. Then sometimes my phone would emit one weak ring and stop, only to ring again after gathering strength for a while—with nothing to show for it but a buzz that competed with the caller's voice.

Although there existed no Miss Telephone Cooperative, I imagined her face lovely and tanned, and her shoulder strap mended by a safety pin: "Everwhen I wear dis, it tears up on me."

Nevertheless, this same "country" also meant adventure. One day, near a store on Highway 501, I got a whiff of something more natural than pleasant—and what was that screechy braying mixed with thumping? Horses in a burning stable? I saw that the commotion issued from a tractor-trailer backed up to a place marked "Conway Stock Yards." While a bunch of pigs—herd, flock, whatever—wriggled and tumbled, a man in a red cap, jumpsuit, and boots jabbed an electric prod at them while yelling some ritual formula in an attempt to get them from truck to chute.

Chickens would peck and strut just down the street from the new headquarters of Conway National Bank. One day Marge and I pulled into a rather shabby gas station, fittingly labeled AMOC. We greeted the man behind the pumps; "Just a minute," he smiled, "I'm washin' my chickens." Sure enough, he held the water hose in one hand and turned a naked fowl in the other as we bent over to hide our delighted laughter.

~~~

So this was the place we would call home. Having been tree-ripened in hometowns, we both wanted to recapture a sense of permanence. In fact, we badly needed to stop after so much mobility, whether for escape, opportunity, or adventure. I myself had led a seminomadic life by car, bus, ship, train, airplane, and rented truck for fourteen years, since graduating from high school in 1960.

"Where do you stay?"

I had first heard this question in Mississippi, where black people would ask it to mean "Where do you live?" The answer would be something like "I stay in Port Gibson." This bit of dialect had registered upon my ear as quaint at best. Then I encountered it once more as Standard Horry: "Oh, you stay over in Red Hill." But by now the formula had a charm to it, even a certain logic. After all, can one *live* completely without *staying?* Without experiencing continuity of place? For such a constant heightens the pleasure of rhythms and diminishes the impact of change.

By the time summer came I had jumped into the opaque river water, greatly increasing my speed every time my foot brushed against alligator-whisker-weeds, telling myself that staying, too, can be broadening.

2

"Where Are You From?"

The more I tried to regard this South Carolina town as an end and not as a means, and the more I circumscribed the future by the squiggly, straight, and curved borders of Horry County, the more the memories flooded over from childhood. To look intently at Conway's houses, people, and customs was to look backward, northward, and inward. As I gazed across the latitudes and decades, I began to appreciate how fully a person can be *from* a place. And after all these years, to my surprise, I would evidently measure my degree of belonging by the place where I had "stayed" — like one of the boulders that marked the driveway across the street in Glen Ellyn, Illinois.

The difference between these two towns could be gauged even by such a prosaic item as the truck. It was ubiquitous in Conway, from our next-door-neighbor's pipe-laden model, to the pickup with cages for hunting dogs, to the occasional panel truck bulging above cars in a driveway, to the tractor-trailer parked next to the highway and measuring a country lot between its front and rear axles, to the block-long vehicle that spewed brown smoke, whirled off pieces of bark, and dangled the driver's old red handkerchief from a log to keep cars from ramming a horizontal forest.

Not that there weren't plenty of imported trucks around

in Glen Ellyn, as I realized one June morning before college. While I waited for the honk of the pickup that would carry me on my first day with a lawn-mowing company, I noticed the husky acceleration of trucks as they furnished the neighborhood with goods and services. But few such vehicles spent the night in town.

This white-collar decorum extended to careers, so that after high school when one parent reported that an acquaintance of mine was driving a truck, the disappointment was palpable. Years later, in New Mexico, I was taken aback when my father-in-law walked out of the office, climbed into his pickup and, still wearing a tie, drove us to Texas for a load of potatoes.

My antisuburbanite Uncle George was about the only person I knew who owned a truck. He lived in a more countrified town on the other line of the Chicago and North Western Railway. When he drove us little cousins home from a movie one night, the hard bed of his pickup bumped us in time to the rattles as the vehicle made its own breeze. Uncle George was never the "organization man." He swore volubly in a sharp, nasal accent, built a couple of houses by himself, bartered, barbered, and then raised prize canaries in an addition to his mobile home. And near my house he did the most un—Glen Ellyn thing I ever witnessed. Returning from a jaunt downtown, his old wood-sided station wagon clattered along Pennsylvania Avenue next to the tracks and then slowed behind a dawdler, and—our car inches forward, violates the civil gap between cars, and clicks against the other bumper, as up flies the driver's hand to hat brim while his disconcerted face swivels between us and the road ahead. "Don't tell your parents," admonishes my uncle as he pushes the man even with the ice plant, disengages, and turns up Kenilworth with his marveling confederate.

16

It was from this Jefferson Ice Company in Glen Ellyn that a red tractor-trailer emerged toward Kenilworth Hill one morning on its out-of-town route. Standing next to the curb with my bicycle I saw another boy up in the passenger seat who was no doubt getting to ride with his father. Our eyes met: I glimpsed his dingy-colored woolen jacket, his worn leather cap, but my feeling of superiority was hard to maintain from down below and left behind, and I thought that he, too, sensed how completely that cab window separated us.

A truck was as much for fun as business. After a high school formal, Tom Hollinger and I surprised our dates by escorting them from the hilltop circle drive into the back of an old panel truck; chauffeured by an employee of the Hollingers' small factory, it groaned off toward the pizza parlor. Even in that summer lawn-mowing job, my friend and I got a kick out of shifting gears on the old pickup while guzzling soda pop and listening to the radio. One of the high points of my boyhood was riding in an old milk truck bought from the dairy by my young neighbor. If it once lost momentum, it stalled, so around the corner we lurched and up the rise, while the outrageously unmuffled engine chugged and cranked so loud we had to yell at each other as we stood laughing in the cab. "YOU'LL HAVE TO JUMP!" he yelled to me, so eyeing a patch of parkway in front of my house, I leaped onto its grass in a run, careful not to trip on the roots of the big cottonwood.

My block of Cottage Avenue was emphasized as a unit by the T-intersections at both ends. West meant toward the corner at Kenilworth. Late one summer afternoon I faced that direction from the crest of my street as the inclining sun made the concrete gleam in a yellow that could have inspired L. Frank Baum to write about Oz. Beyond the field stood a line of tall, narrow poplars that, always unusual in form, now shimmered half-incandescent, symbols of the unknown that beckoned far beyond them.

At the end of brief December afternoons I could sit at a plate of almond crescent cookies and gaze through both regular and storm window past the raggedy-shoveled sidewalk, tinted blue-gray, over the reddish-pink snow, far to the southwest. There, all the heat of the world had contracted to a luminous ball that silhouetted a row of Osage orange trees bordering a lot on the hill crest. Their leafless trunks, branches, and vines wound in a black tangle that burned without being consumed.

Because of the trees, the other end of the block offered little horizon. It was toward the corner at Newton that I watched out the living room window for my dad as he walked home from the train station; from that direction, years later, the car pool would draw up each night. At dawn in summer a large, curly-barked cherry tree outside the east bedroom sketched branches on the glowing window shade.

The house faced south. Yards and vacant lots sloped that way toward Pennsylvania Avenue and the tracks. Although on a sunny winter day the front-porch icicles dripped brilliantly off the roof overhang, those on the back roof looked grayly there to stay. On the ground the shadow of the house allowed enough snow to remain for us to take many an extra turn down the sled-slide my father once built us. In summer, above the tall bushes that separated our back yard from the one behind it, the northern lights sometimes glimmered ethereally.

~~~~

People living in Glen Ellyn moved away so seldom as to give an illusion of permanence. And most of the dozen original houses, plus a half-dozen newer ones that transformed vacant lots into homes, had a rather benevolent air.

On the Munsons' front steps I whiled away a summer hour flipping the pages of comic books. In their living room I watched "The Lone Ranger," taking my Indian name from one program before galloping down the sidewalk to Glen Ellyn's first Indian Guides meeting. When that same stucco bungalow became the Walmanns', I cavorted grotesquely in the basement to draw a laugh from their daughter, home from a special school in Wisconsin. On their sofa I listened to the comical "Grandma's Lye Soap" record, or watched the rope "rabbit" twist and turn over and under and into the hole as Mr. Walmann tried to teach me enough knots to get my Tenderfoot badge before I shaved. Then Mr. and Mrs. Born began two decades of retirement in the same house. They let me play their baby grand piano, and sounds from a violin sometimes wafted from the living room.

Between this house and ours stood a sort of brown-brick Chicago row house that enjoyed extra yard and a two-car garage. Mr. and Mrs. Kranz already lived there when I arrived in town, and lived there when I departed. Although as a child I once vomited on the porch mat, later they paid me generously to uncover the long driveway with a snow shovel and to tend to the dog when it spent their summer vacation at home in the basement. Back from the Episcopal church, tiny Mrs. Kranz often parked in the street temporarily to avoid maneuvering the car into the drive, then pattered up the walk, as quick as she was short, twisting a handkerchief. Instead of ever complaining that our back door often slammed noisily, she might bring us a coffeecake.

On the east side of us stood the ancient red bricks of the

Raffensparger house. Its slate roof was barnlike, with two pitches on each side. In the spare room upstairs I slept the night for several months, after a fire at our place.

Across the street stood a tall white frame house with enclosed porches on the east side of both stories. The Lowdens actually had a maid, perhaps a distant relative. In the basement the sons showed me how a flame could melt dimes illegally; on the sidewalk how a magnifying glass could set a leaf smoking; and on my front porch, how an "I-dare-you" BB pellet, even when shot from the opposite sidewalk, could sting.

Then the Thomsons moved in and stayed for more than twenty years, until long after I had departed. As a baby-sitter I spent several New Year's Eves in their living room reading *Punch* or looking through inherited medical books. In the basement Mr. Thomson occasionally trained his Ph.D. onto my algebra assignment while interrupting his wood-working project. Once, when I painted their kitchen ceiling, the color brightened from one wall to the other like a sunrise because I hadn't mixed the paint well, but no recriminations followed. Although Mr. Thomson's shaggy eyebrows, piercing eyes, and aquiline nose had once caused a child on the bus to burst into tears, we knew him more for his gentle humor and his heartily sung rendition of "Abdul the Bulbul Ameer."

When I came home from school in the afternoons, Mrs. Thomson often sat at our kitchen table with my mom—like her, she called me "Ran." A witty remark would cause her to swing her head downward and sideways and laugh while she spewed cigarette smoke from the corner of her mouth. Once she told me, "That's a non sequitur," and had to provide an explanation. Coffee time or cocktail hour over, this tall woman would walk back across the street with a slight loping motion.

Just before I went off to college, she took me downtown and bought me a handsome sport coat.

To be sure, the neighbors found reasons to reproach me: "Since Eric still believes in Santa Claus, please do not tell him those things anymore." "Did you write your initials in my new cement?" ("No, I think it was Ronny Westrom.") "Wells, was that you who whistled past my bedroom window at 11:00 P.M.?" "Ran, what are you doing brushing your teeth in the kitchen sink!" Firmness was certainly in order for a boy who introduced himself to Mrs. Munson by a slight noise in her kitchen, a glare, and a demand, "WHERE IS RICHARD!?" Because she would not allow me to indulge a nervous habit of clearing my throat, I had to excuse myself and go outside for a good scrape. Her pleasantly solid build and tightly wound braids reflected a disinclination to doubt. Today she might have been a lawyer or executive, but back then she helped manage the large day-care center known as the neighborhood.

~~~

Enclosing the 300 block of Cottage Avenue was the northwest quarter of town. It included Hawthorne School (named for the author); the rear playground was obstructed and graced by a timeless hawthorn whose uniquely wide-rambling branches were off-limits to generations of climbers. The street immediately north of us was Hawthorn, then came Linden, Maple, Oak, and Elm in a natural succession. Paralleling Cottage to the south were Anthony and Pennsylvania.

An irregular grid pattern had been imposed upon the town's slightly rolling contours. So a person walking to the business section jogged slightly up here, there gently subsided, at a corner lot took a dirt hypotenuse that curved outward just a bit—in a rhythm that I could still sense much later, from faraway Conway, much as a sailor who steps onto shore still feels the boat rock.

The corners of Main and Pennsylvania were marked by the post office, a vacant lot that gave rise to the new fire station, Sears & Roebuck, and Kipke's Bakery (whose back door was entered by early-morning paperboys holding six cents for a warm pastry). A block's walk between mostly two-story buildings, by Paul's Shoe Repair and Skate Sharpening, by Heintz's Drug Store (above which lived my fifth-grade teacher), by Patches' Hardware, led to Crescent Boulevard and the tracks. On this corner stood the three-story DuPage Trust Company. From it projected an ornate clock whose pyramidal brass top had turned green and whose hands told many a commuter whether he had that spare minute. Across Main, high archwork adorned the concrete facade of the Professional Arts Building, which looked even more substantial than the bank. A bank it had once been, in fact, and now was somewhat incongruously occupied by Walgreen's Drug Store on the ground floor at the corner. Across the tracks lay another block or so of Main Street businesses and apartments, equally well-kept and even boasting a stretch of Tudor facades. The business section ended abruptly at Hillside Avenue across from the lawn of the Episcopal church, where several black metal hitching posts lined the curb as relics of the past.

The next sphere encompassed the rest of Glen Ellyn. Next came the outskirts of ragweed and prairie, and of houses surrounded by yards full of dandelions and plantain weeds. Next came the farms lying past Roosevelt Road (Route 30) at the south, and North Avenue (Route 64) at the north, both of which extended straight east into Chicago.

The next sphere held my relatives' homes. Near the Fox River my cousins' yard contained earthworms for fishing, a snake hutch, a beehive, and at one time a horse. Spectators would hold their breath as my cousin leapt from the railroad bridge into the river. My dad's sister, although ample, could somehow float motionlessly, her eyes closed, her smile like Mona Lisa's.

Adjacent to Chicago lived my cousin Joan Wells, whose old neighborhood had no driveways to add that precious space between houses; instead, houses had an alley behind them. Also in Oak Park lived my mother's parents, first with Great Grandma Capps in a brick house with plates on the dining room wall and a boulevard nearby that stirred me with its hum of cars and buses; then in an apartment that had a vulgar-sounding buzzer to unlock the front door, a bed that folded into the wall, and Jack Benny's voice on the radio making my grandfather chuckle as he smoked his pipe.

~~~

Many natives would come back frequently to this haven, either in fact or in memory. Tom Hollinger and I would even return to it from the west after setting off toward the east on a journey around the globe. As a sojourner I would always look to Glen Ellyn as my base. But could someone become like an odd jazz pianist who could play in only one key? Could a person improvise on the same root chords too often? After making progression after progression upon them, could this musician have trouble beginning over in a new home key?

Now poising my Zebco fishing rod, I made another cast into the Waccamaw, wondering if "Where Are You From?" could interfere with "Where Do You Stay?"

3

Into the Thick of Things

The time was coming for us to move from the river —from "Savannah Bluff" in the "Red Hill" area, as natives called it, although I had yet to spy any kind of swelling, and the nearest hill of any size was in Hamlet, North Carolina. Certainly we enjoyed our rented cottage, upon which we had hung a string of red chilies brought from New Mexico (which soon molded in the damp air). We certainly had nothing against our neighbor ("Oh, you stay next to Brother Black"). Nor did we unduly fear the Apennine-spined alligator that was reported to sashay up the river. But I was no longer in the mood to live near house trailers. Like my trailer in Connecticut, which had figuratively carried me to a master's degree, these were means, not ends. Moreover, we wanted to live in the town proper, and were ready to trade a measure of adventure for one of involvement. And we wanted to live in our own house, and on our own land.

Just to drive over to our property on the other side of town brought us pleasure. We would cross the river on the Highway 501 Bypass, then travel along a causeway next to a lake carved out of the swamps and used as a cooling pond by the big power plant across the highway.

A right turn onto Highway 378 (Third Avenue) led us to

its terminus in downtown Conway. At Third and Main we would admire the handsome, two-story wooden clock tower. The clock itself was not so much reliable as venerable. City hall, beside it, was originally built as a courthouse in 1825, under the design of Robert Mills, architect of the Washington Monument. Staircases on each side of the facade led to the second-floor portico. The four large wooden columns were painted white, and pocked with irregular, shallow shapes that made my palms want to rub them. Hands had not only laid the bricks but made them, judging from their slight variations.

That the building across the street could exhibit decayed window frames in its upper story annoyed me, as did the billboards on the next corner at Main and Fourth. Yet the downtown did impart the sense of a hub, albeit a rusty one.

At the next corner, Main and Fifth Avenue, stood the post office. Cousin to Glen Ellyn's in architecture, it was flanked by a pair of live oaks to make a composition of leaves, bricks, bark, fanlights, mortar, moss, and shadows that might be titled "Institutions." To the left, down Fifth, one could glimpse the Horry County Memorial Library, part homey, part classic, inviting the reader to the front door between its two wings. Another block down Fifth, past Laurel, would lead to Elm Street, which contracted to a single lane around an oak that itself bifurcated into two tree-sized trunks. We continued down Main and passed near to where Sixth Street divided around the oasis of another oak, which shaded a monument to Confederate soldiers.

Within a half mile of this marker were sprinkled large ancestral homes. The air-conditioning system of one wide house comprised high ceilings, broad porches, and the branches of a live oak that somehow reached past both ends of the place. Among these civic prizes were interspersed more

modest houses, many with long, anachronistic porches on which citizens had once taken refuge from the heat. Newer neighborhoods, usually without sidewalks, leapfrogged over the plywood mill and curtain factory on the former edge of town. The black sections — with their housing projects, their small lots, and their houses whose sides often needed painting and sometimes failed to make a forty-five-degree angle with the roof line — lay near the V made by Highways 501 and 378.

Turning right onto one of the streets with "Lake" in its

name (I had trouble distinguishing among several in that area), we passed the chapel-like Episcopal church, then entered a tunnel of trunks and canopies made by water oaks, crossed the railroad track, then continued down another "Lake" street. It made a bend under moss-draped limbs. Then we turned right onto Long Avenue, which curved through the swamp like the elongated S of the Studebaker insignia, crossed the mud-bottomed canal, and emerged next to a small farm on the right.

Then we turned left onto Golf Club Road. Before making a quick right onto our street, we could see far ahead to where the Club Road crossed the railroad track by the hardwood mill, which sometimes sent a great white puff of steam floating across the road. Turning down Graham Road, unmarked and unpaved, we drove down the ruts, and then parked. We searched for our property, which, with the lot beyond it, helped make up the corner of the city.

The stakes finally discovered, I tried connecting them with string, but briars and thickets made the lines roll, tangle and bulge. Prickers that bit like baby snakes drew the wrath of my bush axe. But we began to distinguish some fairly large pines, found that we did indeed own a handsome oak, judged those other trees to be maples, and, look here—a holly tree! Another discovery was a V-shaped pine, which caused us to set the proposed house back five feet.

For help in our appraisal we asked Professor Joe Pinson to take us on our own field trip. He taught us to distinguish between a red maple and a sweet gum, pronounced our favorite tree a post oak, classified that one as a willow oak (contrary to the Illinois rule that an oak has lobed leaves), and identified the holly as a female that would produce red berries. He also pointed out a jessamine vine, a huckleberry bush, gallberry bushes, even a little bay tree, and myrtle bushes: "Smell this," he urged, breaking off some leaves that cleared our sinuses.

~~~

Out in the community, too, we continued to get a sense of things, even to shape them a bit. Marge delivered many a newborn native in the old Conway Hospital. As for my own work, I had longed for centrality but had become centrifugal. As an extension teacher for the college I taught airmen at Myrtle Beach Air Force Base, seniors at Myrtle Beach High School (both at the beach where a few of my students took an autumn vacation when the tourist season ended), and students at a technical school located sixty-five miles away. Driving back one night I almost hit the fat silhouette of a pig.

In town I wrote a column for the *Field & Herald,* and served as temporary chairman of the Chamber of Commerce's Beautification Committee, helping to get an ordinance written against storing junked cars in plain view.

Marge and I started square dancing. I had learned this activity in the basement of Hawthorne School. Now, in the cafeteria of another grade school, the crowd circled, shuffled, promenaded, passed through, boxed the gnat, wove the ring, the whole dance a loom of people, thousands of hands touching in a night, farmers and townspeople crossing, male and female, children and grownups allemanding left, bouncing, sweating, laughing—as when the caller told the men to "Swing that pretty little taw in front of you" and I found myself staring at a concrete block wall.

Invited to join one of the civic clubs that were so prominent in the social fabric, I gratefully accepted. Every Friday the Lions ate lunch, sang, joked, and listened to a presentation that had some bearing on the community. I had wanted to join one ever since Vicksburg, where I had spent many an hour in town studying, hiking, sketching—and noticing other men "Hello!" each other.

Lion Randy did draw the line at singing "Our Boys Will Shine Tonight," in honor of the high school football team. I simply mumbled, never quite certain whether it was "When the moon goes down and the sun comes up" or "When the sun goes down and the moon comes up." But I would belt out "She'll Be Comin' 'round the Mountain," and once offered a symbolic exegesis of each stanza so that guests would not mistake it for a piece of nonsense. I not only enjoyed the group, but needed its help. Since I belonged to no church, that foothold so valuable to a newcomer, especially in the South, the Lions' meeting room at the Conway Motor Inn was the closest thing to the fellowship hall of the Congregational Church back in Glen Ellyn.

Gathering at that restaurant were forty-five men of assorted ages and careers: Lion John, who was my sponsor and a heating-and-cooling expert; the young banker from downriver in Toddville; the chain-smoking lawyer, one of many professionals in the area who had studied mainly in South Carolina; Billy Joe Calhoun, who with other family members owned the Red & White grocery next to the Episcopal church; the chiropractor from Iowa who had recruited five hundred eye donors, and possessed strong arms but walked with a cane as a result of polio; the crane-factory comptroller, one of the Catholic imports, whose tough Brooklyn brogue was belied by his fun-loving temperament; the undertaker, Lion Mac Goldfinch, a director of the National Eye Bank; the jeweler who inherited his father's store on Main; the stout county auditor, who invited Marge and me for coffee at his house full of Clemsoniana; the probate judge, an acute septuagenarian; the genial part-time preacher who worked for the Telephone Cooperative, a fact that tempered my feelings toward that outfit; and Ezel "Skeets" Solomon, who had owned a department store downtown, and who could be counted on to stand up and regale us with a joke enhanced by his curly white hair, black-framed glasses, and nasal drawl. I was always intrigued by the idea of Southern Jews (a few of whom lived in Conway) because I always associated them with Northern cities.

At each meeting, Lioness Rod McCown brought her upbeat energy to the piano. Her husband, Lion Harold, always sat in the far corner smoking; the beloved principal of Burroughs School, he was now retired and in precarious health. Following Rule 9B of small towns, the McCowns lived next door to someone whom Marge and I knew: the obstetrician who had invited her to come to Conway and work for him.

The various projects undertaken by the Lions also helped me to make a path into the community. We recruited eye donors, tended the Salvation Army kettle at Christmas, and sold brooms house to house in spring.

This knocking on doors brought back the sharp ear for sounds within a house that I had developed as a paperboy. One door was opened by a fellow square dancer, one doorbell summoned a student of mine. I laughed with a woman whose grandson "is always standing up for some things but can't stand others — like a broom"; I talked with a ninety-seven-year-old man whose daughter, my colleague, had taken Marge and me on a hunt for Venus flytraps. Once I carried my wares down a half-concealed street with quite modest houses — but look at the thriving vegetable rows, and across from them that fountain of roses! When a family of gardeners declined to buy a broom, mop, or a light bulb, I vowed, "Next year I'll sell you a shovel!" Once a resident asked, "How did a Yankee like you get to Conway?" "Just good luck," I returned.

One Friday evening, who should turn up at the football game but Lion Randy, not to watch our boys shine but to help run the concession stand. I studied the customers as they fixed their eyes behind me upon a treasury of goodies, brightly packaged and many-shaped, as various as themselves. There was a man with ladderlike calluses on his fingers and palms, as if he used his hands for wrenches. Other hands were delicate and their nails polished; they belonged to some of the white girls who wore ample makeup and chic clothes and who spoke with a kind of sweet intonation. These belles had their contraries in some of the black girls, who seemed a little tough. If the first sort of girl was a hothouse flower, the second was clearly a sturdier variety.

~~~

All this grounding in both land and community was natural to me, but was now also vital. I needed to dig in quickly and deeply. Apparently fixed in Conway, was I still not skidding through? Now and then a trace of that utter disorientation returned that had attacked me the night I had unloaded our rented truck in Mississippi. My eyes had opened upon lamplit stimuli with no shape or purpose, no field against ground, as in a panic I tried to force a sense of up, down, where, what. In Conway these little spells also resembled my brother Dudley's experience in the air force:

> When I was going TDY from Alaska to England or Okinawa, I found myself on a different continent every night. Sometimes I didn't know where I was—no roots whatsoever. I had absolutely no biorhythms and was fifteen hours out of synch with the sun clock. While flying, I could be anywhere. I was utterly detached, with no windows; our only contact with the

earth was by radio, which was all-directional, so we didn't know where signals came from unless we identified ourselves. Instead of living in a place where you think of yourself as a guy who lives here and walks down this street, you have only a digital readout that tells you exactly where you are and exactly what time it is.

Despite occasional fits of disconnection, I kept trying to think of myself as a guy who "stayed" in the place.

4

Railroads

When we drove through Conway, I had an instinctive fear of railroad crossings with no gates or bells or lights. The mere wooden X suggested the skull-and-cross-bones flag. I always stopped, looked, and listened, having grown up on a trunk line rather than a branch line.

Although Horry County was almost four times the size of DuPage County in Illinois, there was only a solitary pair of tracks stretching through its pines to end at the beach. Now and then a Seaboard Coast Line train would announce itself by a prolonged blast, a lantern man would station himself in the intersection, and a locomotive would inkle-dinkle anti-climactically over the single track, pushing or pulling a half-dozen cars heaped with wood chips from the hardwood mill or coal for the generating plant. Ultimately I broke myself of the habit of looking both ways after a train had just vacated the single track. I began merely to pause at the sign, then charge through, just as most residents did. But my anxious uncertainty marked me as more tourist than native. The informal rail crossings seemed to define not only Conway but, in pointed contrast, a place that I found myself recalling more and more often, where town and track had been inseparable.

The railroad had antedated Glen Ellyn. In 1851, Dr. Lewey

Q. Newton, a landowner, "believing that a thriving town could be built if once started, obtained a promise of the railroad company to stop their trains providing a depot was put up without cost to them."* He was right, and the center of population eventually moved there from the stagecoach line a mile northward.

A hundred years later it was still a kind of railroad town. Not that one ever saw striped caps and blue overalls, as in Laramie, with its train yard and its tie-creosoting plant. But looking back homeward at the railroad from the vantage point of Conway, I sorted out various feelings that it brought to our daily life. They were centrality, security, danger, and adventure.

～～～

Glen Ellyn shared the railroad ambience of the urban North. Not until I moved south did I realize how many bumpy train crossings a driver made in the Chicago area. My father not only took the train to the city, but then walked through a railroad yard as a shortcut to Montgomery Ward & Company's headquarters. In the morning I would half listen to my mother's "400 Hour," a radio program of classical music sponsored by the Chicago and North Western—400 being the number of miles and minutes it took their northbound streamliners to reach Minneapolis. And among our early neighbors, Mr. Impey worked as an inspector for Electro-Motive, which manufactured diesel-electric locomotives; and Don Raffensparger headed the baggage and express department of the Chicago, Burlington and Quincy Railroad in Chicago. Just north of the city limits the Great

*Blythe P. Kaiser and Dorothy I. Vandercook, *Glen Ellyn's Story: and her neighbors in DuPage.* 1976, p. 46.

Northern, mysterious of name, hauled freight to unknown destinations.

Right through the middle of our town ran not one railroad but three: the Chicago, Aurora & Elgin; the Chicago and North Western; and the Union Pacific (which used the tracks of the North Western). The five tracks were divided by a wide median into one set of three and one of two. A pedestrian might traverse these five tracks at several ground-level crossings in the business district, or via a single-lane underpass farther east.

The trains were our industry. Into the lovely town they exploded like a male force. Multiple engines trundled through, churning out smoke and pulling boxcars that wore the colors of railroads from all over the U.S. and Canada, as well as tank cars, refrigerator cars, flat cars, latticed live-stock cars, auto racks, hopper cars, gondola cars, often more than a hundred at a time, carrying goods to or from Chicago. Interstate passenger trains charged toward or from the West, as unlikely as the freights to stop at our station, whose existence they acknowledged merely by a "LOOK OUT!" blast of the air horn.

Like the streamliners and freights, the commuter trains, pulled by immense steam locomotives, made us feel near the center of things. They evoked the power, the dispatch, the consequence and impersonality of the invisible city twenty miles away. A blazing light rounding the curve two miles east of the platform meant Dad: but gradually materializing about the light was a black cylinder that hurtled to the coasting point just before Park Boulevard, rolled through the crossing, still at fearsome speed, slowed, and now hissed, clunked, and screeched past heavily, its spokes, rods, pipes, rivets, boiler, and funnels admitting no distinction between outer surface and inner machinery, its drive wheels taller than a man.

The Chicago, Aurora & Elgin used electric power. This kind of train made no distinction between engine and car, for whichever unit came first led. While the train rested at the station it went pumpa-pumpa-pumpa, a sound which I always assumed meant a storing-up of electricity. Archaic-looking, often shabby, with wooden trim inside, the string of red and gray-blue cars did not seem intimidating like the North Western's long dingy-brown cars and cinder-showering locomotives.

If a person took the electric "Roar'n Elgin" eastward, it

would pass through suburbs, plunge past laundry hung behind depressing slum tenements, then finally graze the sooty buildings next to the elevated tracks which defined Chicago's "Loop." But get on a westbound, and once past Wheaton the train would zip right through prairies like a trolley on a country holiday.

As the electric railroad declined, eventually to follow its gate man and his tower into history, the North Western prospered. Commuter trains were now pulled by diesel engines— I saw my first one while playing Little League baseball at Memorial Park—and the smoky cars gave way to snappy new ones, double-decker to boot. As if salvaging something from the electric railway, the eastbound trains traveled backwards, guided by an engineer in the front car and pushed by the engine.

~~~

The train was not only a quickening force in Glen Ellyn, but a stabilizing one. Its recurrence, though semirandom, was a constant in life. Back and forth it passed, night and day. Our own interrupted mobility was a reminder of local citizenship: Ding! ding! ding! and the crossing gate jerks and lowers, lights flash; how long will we have to sit? "Oh, no, a freight!" The engines lumber into sight, expelling brown exhaust, and we begin to review the Gross National Product. At last the crossing is clear again, rather strangely empty and still after all that mass, speed, and color. Then our bike or car climbs the slight rise of the embankment to thunk over the spaces between rails and wood.

A North Western local stopped at Glen Ellyn every hour during the day, and a cluster of commuter expresses arrived early in the morning and again in the evening, when onto the platform streamed hundreds of men and a sprinkling of women. For many a family, the times of departure and arrival supplied basic terms for life's equation. The touch of the platform under the business shoe must have meant Home Again to many a commuter.

A few mornings when our car arrived late at the station, my mother had to "race the train." For me such a phrase, such an event, violated the strict decorum that governed the town's relationship with the railroad. I imagined the great locomotive running boiler-to-hood with our car as my mother, clad in a houserobe, gunned it past the forest preserve to the Lombard station, the squealing tires making the conductor turn and look as he swung onto the already moving steps.

Another breach of railway ritual occurred some years later. Because of a train wreck on the Chicago, Burlington and Quincy line, which ran about ten miles south of town, a Burlington train was routed over the North Western tracks. Not yellow but silver, the coaches glided slowly through town, dome by dome, a sight as amazing as if the electric train had jumped over to the regular tracks. By what spurs, by what creeping through mazes of freight yards, by what rusty switches, had this linkage been made possible?

In my earliest memories the trains figure. A penny placed on the rail would be flipped off by the locomotive wheel to become curved, thin and warm as if molded against the palate: Lincoln gum. I was so young when my father took me on an excursion to Wheaton that as we walked home from the station I could point to a dark house on Cottage and declare, "A witch lives there." Returning from Oak Park one winter night on the CA&E, I sat drowsily with my parents in the front car. It stood, halted, somewhere in the dark, warmed by a potbelly stove. Finally the conductor or driver broke the silence: "Waiting for a freight—the tracks cross at ground level here."

My grandfather Capps took me to Elgin on the electric train to see his mother in the nursing home. It was the last time I saw her, as she reached over the quilt to pat me, and the only time I remember. On the way home, as my grandfather and I sat in the smoking compartment, a weathered woman across from us asked him, "How long have you smoked a pipe?"—and resumed puffing on her own.

The train brought continuity not only from youth to age but from day to night. The end of many a day was signaled by a great CHUFF that reached my south bedroom somewhat muffled from the station a mile or so away. Then came a momentary chattering of lesser ones, followed by slow, determined chuffs that accelerated to a hammering of almost imperceptible intervals, the noise now passing directly south of me, ever so gradually diminishing to the west and to the plains of sleep.

∿∿∿

If they lent a stabilizing force, the trains were nevertheless our constant civic danger. The third rail made even silence sinister. A person who traversed the CA&E crossing could eye that bar of gray steel that ran parallel to the outside rail of both sets of tracks and stuck up a little higher than the other rails. On the first day of junior high school I asked a student if her street wasn't near where the boy had been killed by the third rail. "That was my brother," she replied.

As for the coal- or oil-powered trains nearby, we kids would watch respectfully as each freight car far above leaned slightly toward us, the rails that were supposed to support and guide it now bowing upward as the middle of the car passed, to be slapped down again by each clanking pair of wheels. Or we listened to the rumbling crescendo of an engine and saw it burst into view from the west, canted toward us as it

39

rounded the slight bend through town, and then opened its throttle on the straightaway. Partly because of this curve we did not have much of a view at two of the crossings. A train horn blasted out the long-long-short-long series which meant "approaching a crossing," but from which direction? Or would two trains appear? Even three? When a trio did try to share the roadbed simultaneously, the onlookers (and perhaps the engineers) could only hold their breath.

Things were tricky at the North Western station. Because trains rode on the left-hand track, British style, we had to take care when leaning over the platform for a better view. When a local pulled away, we dared not cross until the bell on the wooden pedestrian crossway stopped clanging. "If you see the train coming at you," the saying went, "you can't move out of the way," and who had not rehearsed this fatal paralysis in imagination or dream? When a steam locomotive thundered aggressively, almost angrily, through town, how did the long steel rods shuttle in such a blur without flying off the wheels, the wheels not melt the tracks, the whole black, smoke-spouting vision not go berserk?

Although the train took fathers from families temporarily, one took family from father permanently. When I was about seven years old a locomotive hit a car and killed the mother and her two daughters. A memorial service was held at Hawthorne School by Rev. Mr. J. Stanley Stevens, my minister, as we sat cross-legged on the squares of the basement auditorium. The girls had been another schoolmate's cousins, and one day I saw a taxi stop at her house and let out a solitary man who carried his suitcases up the walk. I whispered the tragic family's name—one that would always evoke the sundering that might result from transgressing upon our most public of systems.

Our town could not ignore the possibility of another kind

of railroad accident. One evening as I searched for an errant baseball in the vines around the Raffenspargers' house, somebody asked my dad, "Did you hear about the train wreck?" The phrase struck my ears as "earthquake" or "forest fire" might to a child in another region. As the two talked about the derailed freight, my grassy yard seemed a bit smaller and the dusk less benign. Every few years after that, another freight tested its wheels on the bare ground. The image of such derailment was my vision of chaos: a chain of cars splitting into links, containers merging with contents, fresh produce made garbage, couplers now battering rams, corners now plows, the guiding rails themselves thrashing like injured snakes.

In the eighth grade, I went to Wheaton to view the infamous fifty-six-car train wreck. From an overpass I looked up to the top of a pile of freight cars so high as to seem dropped out of the sky one by one. For a week special trains bore wreckage through our town like armaments destroyed in a great, lost battle.

Yet the routine reestablished itself and, as usual, neither the certainties of the third rail nor the dubious physics of the regular type bothered us much. On Monday nights in high school, walking to my piano lesson, I would even dare a shortcut across both sets of tracks. At that point there was a break in the third rail through which I entered the first track; then walking down the ties, I reached a break in a middle electric rail; negotiating it, I turned back along the other track to a break in the outer third rail, where I exited. On my way home I would again make this capital N, taking great care to keep my balance on the ties and to stay alert for any lightninglike glimmer of electricity on the horizon, a low groan of motor and wheels, a faint gleam of a headlight —knowing, however, that if a train should appear I could retrace or complete the maze in enough time, albeit with a pounding heart and a wrinkled copy of Bartok's *Microkosmos*.

A few years before my move to Conway a freight train in Glen Ellyn did derail across from the former Ice Plant and spew poison gas over the neighborhood. My father rode around like Paul Revere to help sleeping people evacuate the area, and on the national news St. Petronelle's Catholic Church was named as a refugee center. Touring the area on a visit home, I noted the new rails and roadbed, the burned-up weeds alongside them, and the crease along Pennsylvania Avenue made by a boxcar. But the only railroad mishap in which I was ever involved occurred when the car of my dairy-truck friend bumped over the Great Western crossing, knocked out a kingpin, crashed onto the pavement, and slid almost into the yard of the Hollingers' factory.

~~~

So all these things—centrality, security, and danger—were represented by the train. But it also meant adventure.

Paradoxically, living so near the city of Chicago, we could still feel somewhat provincial as a shiny streamliner charged through with its ten long cars—mail, baggage, diner, coach, and Pullman. We had to move our heads just to read "The City of Omaha" or "The City of Portland" or to glimpse a corner of white linen tablecloth in the yellow streak. Although these "Cities" became truncated and eventually disappeared, they kept the idea before us of distant places.

Even the local trains could bring excitement, especially if one's parents forbade an out-of-town jaunt without permission. Every so often I would buy a ticket in the North Western station, a sort of railroad museum with its hard benches, heavy wooden trim, high ceilings, and green-visored agent. With my ticket in hand I would climb aboard and soon watch the library pass by at Park Boulevard, then the cannons in Memorial Park, then the high school crowning its hill. After stopping at a few towns, the long car would pass alongside a bottomless quarry and then through endless rail yards with signs that warned "No Humping." Then came square miles of factories and warehouses. As the train slowed near the terminal, the white buildings of Montgomery Ward & Company could be glimpsed beyond the rail yards that my father hiked as a shortcut to work.

On the way home the conductor ritually proclaimed each step of the way: "KEDzie. . . . OAK Park. . . . MAYwood. . . . ELLUMhurst. . . . VILLA Park. . . . LUMbard. . . ." A momentary rumbling meant that the train had crossed a sort of drawbridge over the DuPage River. "GLEN Ellyn. GLEN Ellyn next."

Occasionally such trips were sanctioned by parents, as when I visited my cousin Joan, or carried an eyeglass prescription or a forgotten briefcase to a particular stop in the Loop. But usually uncountenanced, they seemed a bit gamy, even to the potent Coca-Cola mixed in the CA&E station by holding the cup under the syrup nozzle but tipping it away from the soda-water nozzle prematurely.

A couple of times a buddy and I took the "Roarin' Elgin" to Aurora. There the Burlington Road had a rail yard where we looked up at the silver engines that throbbed with a continental magnitude.

~~~~

Hour by hour, day by day, year by year, the bells would clang, the gates lower, the trains stop or sweep through. Looking back from a river town, I wondered how many of us had even understood how the wheels stayed on the narrow rails. I myself had assigned it partly to custom.

43

5

~~~

Adventures in Not Moving

———

W hat's down at the end of Graham Road?" I wondered aloud. Soon we were walking past a few
houses apparently built a couple of decades before, then a
dilapidated barn surrendered to vines, then a modest house
on a lot that barely staved off the field rising on three of its
sides. This vegetation, along with the tall, full oak, two
pecan trees (not peeKAHN but PEEkan), a middling magnolia, and two rows of cedars, somehow blended with a
pickup, a boat or two, assorted boards, cases of empty soda-
pop bottles stacked halfway up on an old shed, some kind of
coop, a great wooden spool, one or two wrecked cars, and a
disused rusty oil barrel. Past this homestead the road became
the driveway to a cabinlike house almost overgrown by trees
and bushes.

"Graham," read Marge from the mailbox, causing the
guardian roosters to chase us away. But what a pleasure to
find that we lived on an authentic road, an indigenous road.
The subdivisions outside of town, by contrast, named streets
after colleges or members of the developer's family.

Once I crossed Graham and followed a path through the
woods to a pasture, then around its end, where I picked and
pushed my way through bushes, vines, and briars—to dis-
cover a virgin hardwood swamp. I stood there among ferns

44

and great trunks, with no signs of modern civilization, not even a still-smoking Indian campfire. When our farmer-neighbor offered some manure to fertilize my ivy, I took a cart to the pasture and, like an initiate, pushed through the squalid, fly-covered burlap bag into the horse stall.

I might see this lanky farmer in the morning as he strode along in boots, swinging a big can of fresh milk, dog trotting behind. In the evening he might walk his cattle back from pasture to barn. These ancient scenes stirred me. And I felt he valued his work for more than practical reasons. Once, for example, I noticed him standing amid his crop of beans and inspecting a harplike arrangement of wires and stakes, his hands carefully making adjustments on the shoulder-high plants that twined on the wires. "The artist figure of the farmer," as William Carlos Williams wrote.

In town I came upon an overgrown nature trail and near it an abandoned old fire engine, much begadgeted, reposing half-concealed in its own memory garden. "I admire you," declared another newcomer, whom I had told about this find, "for the knack you have for getting into the place." But although enjoying my investigations, I also recognized myself as a Johnny-come-lately.

My outsider status was rubbed in one day behind an automobile body shop. (My car had been rammed while I was riding the circuit for the college.) As I labored to raise the big overhead door, tugging at one handle, twisting another— out popped a man from a small door within the big one. I had been knocking on the wrong door. Anyone from around there would have known better. I remembered the night Tom and I had slipped into Chicago on the train and then boarded a bus, whose driver rebuked me when I stepped down at the rear exit and unwittingly triggered a signal to stop.

Here in Conway I wondered how could so many cars run

around with dealer's license plates? Why was the drivers license bureau impossible to reach by car? Perhaps because it was located at the irrational corner of Third and Fourth avenues? As for the streets, why did the state own and maintain 70 percent of them in town? Nor could I understand one railroad crossing, which I named the Octopus: five different roads or halves of roads met at the tracks, but one of them had no stop sign at either side, so at the junction a driver had to look out for a train and simultaneously watch for vehicles from four other places as well as remember who had the unaccountable right-of-way.

And why were the school buses often driven by students? On a visit to Conway, Tom theorized: "Each morning the kids have a lottery to see who drives." Why did one mechanic not ask the customer's name? "I got your car, don't I?"

At the Lions Club's Ladies Night, Marge and I paraded through the tables late (thanks to someone's new baby). Carrying my bronze-topped flask I looked forward to the zany time promised by several members. "You might want to put that under the table," someone whispered, "there's no drinking."

It didn't take long to realize that "going to Columbia" meant traveling to the state capital rather than attending a university in New York City; that Florence, pronounced Flahrence rather than Flohr-ence, belonged not to Italy but to the next county; and that Georgetown was a place not where congressmen dined but where paper mill employees kept alive a town that had once gotten rich on rice watered by tidal rivers and slave sweat.

But why, when I took my first shower, did I have to step back in to wash off the soap? Why did a person have to dial long distance to reach a certain office in the courthouse? And when I entered the Fisherman's Headquarters, why did all the denizens stop talking?

~~~

We may not have fit in right away, but we enjoyed playing tourist. Marge and I pulled off the road at a fire tower near the college. "Think we can climb it?" I asked. "Well . . . I don't see any 'Keep Off' signs." Up the stairs we bounded, clutching the handrails and making zigzags until we could survey every treetop in the county. The wind whisked Marge's blond hair onto her pink cheek and, less fetchingly, shook the tower's struts. I wondered why, in an age of electronic and aerial surveillance, this structure had not been dismantled. Just for a lark I knocked on the trapdoor above our heads—which opened onto a woman's expressionless face. I could only stammer. Afterward I regretted not saying to the fire watcher, "We're on a scavenger hunt," or "Would you need aluminum siding?"

In downtown Conway we often walked around to shop and explore, perhaps to sip a milkshake at the Horry Drug Store on Main Street. First we would park by the fish market, which backed up to the channel between the Waccamaw and Kingston Lake. This wooden building—how flimsily picturesque it looked under the monumental oak branches. The air announced fried-fish sandwiches in the making. Walking down an alley we could still make out the sign "Colored Cafe" painted on a brick wall. Reaching Main Street we looked across at the Holliday Theatre, owned by tobacco magnates from Galivants Ferry; a separate entrance led to a balcony once filled with black patrons.

Above the drug store was a window with gold letters reading "Dr. J.A. Sasser." This prominent citizen had died twenty years earlier. Now two of his sons were physicians in town and one was a lawyer. Below this window, a plastic proboscis reading "Horry Drugs" stuck out from the old bricks. The entrance was rather inauspicious with its crinkled paint and worn carpet. If this had been Wednesday afternoon, we'd have encountered a locked door without explanation.

Inside, the soda fountain seemed to be marble, or perhaps a marblelike amalgam of stones and minerals, not so much beautiful as solid and genuine. We would go back to a booth. Such space wasters had been yanked out long ago from Heintz's Drug Store in my hometown. There were only two, perhaps the remnant of a full row. Rather uncompromising, these high-backed wooden benches nevertheless offered the most relaxing place in Conway. Although people might go to the new McDonald's because they *lacked* time, people sat here because they *had* some. In fact, at McDonald's the paintings, photographs, and artifacts that hung on the wall to celebrate the area's heritage just pointed up the contrast between extrinsic and intrinsic local. For no amount of maps, potbellied stoves, ship paintings, or oxen yokes could duplicate the unhurried, unspecialized, down-home atmosphere of the drug store and the town.

We admired the lofty ceilings with its white squares, maybe plaster, its rolled borders and wide, ornate plaster molding. Those fluorescent lights were obviously a later addition, unlike the fluorescent panel in McDonald's acoustic-tile ceiling.

The fountain boy was certainly amiable, volunteering to make us a fresh pot of coffee. Up at the fountain we could perhaps hear a Clemson or Carolina football game—a much more natural sound than the canned music or insistent BEEP! BEEP! of the French-fries timer at McDonald's. A humming across the aisle originated from the candy cooler, which held boxes of Nunnally's brand, "The candy of the South." Although the machine called itself a Freshidor, its surface was yellowed and its style of script outdated.

As time passed, one customer stepped back to speak with the pharmacist, another stayed at the fountain, another dropped in and asked for a pipe cleaner, and when he left two ladies entered to settle into a booth. Usually an acquaintance would turn up; in fact somebody had once declared, "If this place closed, I'm afraid I'd never see you again!"

As we waited for our second cup, we appreciated the casual arrangement of the merchandise. Next to the Freshidor stood a display case for batteries; up on the fountain rested a comb display; in the shallow bin to our left, next to the Rhulispray, Rhulicream, and Rhulihist lay a single Frisbee. I myself had bought the other one. What was that indefinite-shaped item on the shelf below? Lookit! (a remnant of my own patois). A Snoopy cookie cutter.

The attendant had to squeeze past a rack full of puzzles by revolving it like a turnstyle. He didn't wear a uniform, and on some afternoons his girlfriend kept him company behind the fountain.

At last it was time to pry ourselves away from our half-secluded trysting place. One of us would point to the old display case for Life Savers candy behind the fountain, or to the old wooden straw-dispenser, the "Schupp's Sani-Straw Miser," or to the pair of Hamilton Beach mixers and metal canisters.

"Y'all come back." We tried to push the door open but it pulled inward.

～～～

The morning air was still too cool to open the pickup's window as a local fellow and I sped along with a borrowed canoe roped to the top.

"That looks like fun," I said.

"What?"

"Those two kids sitting in that little rumble seat behind the tractor."

"They're plantin' tobacco," he said drily. I reconsidered.

At Galivants Ferry we put into the Little Pee Dee next to a general store. With several other canoes, we soon navigated under the Highway 501 bridge with its vehicles thundering to or from the beach. Soon there was no gleam of metal, no litter, no hum of wheels, no right angles. We floated and paddled down a local secret.

As we pulled the base of the paddle and pushed the top, I noticed how the current reflected the trees brokenly, like a painting done with the broad side of a brush and then patted in different colors. For long stretches we needed only to steer around abrupt curves or away from snags for overhanging branches — snake hammocks. Occasionally another canoe would smash into such an overhang, and once both paddlers leaned at the same time only to plunge into the water, surfacing to see their ice chest floating oceanward.

S by S the river parted the wilderness. Cypress trunks, fluted at the bottom, spread at the tops to a squashed triangle of angular branches. These bore green spring leaves, light and dark, as well as swaying moss and bunches of mistletoe like caught tumbleweeds. Red-orange flowers, perhaps from a vine, spread vertically here and there amid the red leaves of the maples, gums, oaks, palisades of saplings, trees extending behind them as far as the eye could probe. Each panorama looked the same, yet different. Sometimes the great cypress trunks would be broken off, some hosted big owl holes, some had thick woody vines running straight up the entire trunk. Some trees stood right in the river. Land, just a bank of sand or dirt, was rarely visible. In the swamp the trees displayed brown high-water rings.

"My grandfather once built two barns made of cypress,"

mused my local companion. But no log truck could get to these expensive trunks safe within their moat.

We occasionally pulled our canoe yard by yard beside a water field of giant pennywort weed (as it seemed to me), each green pad turgid and with roots unseen.

"Do you think they have roots to the bottom or just float?"

"Beats me."

We veered around a snake-shaped snag, bobbing just out of the drink. No water skiers in this river, where ripples could mean the point of a submerged limb. Now and then a creek or slough would run off through the swamp. Once we fought the current to steer in, then clunked against cypress knees, tore spider webs, and tried not to eat branches. "Look! A muskrat! Maybe a beaver!" I caught a glimpse of a furry muzzle that paddled into oblivion.

Sometimes we weren't quite sure which way to go but followed the current, which quickened in the narrow stretches. The element we stirred up and floated upon was all the more mysterious to me because no rain had fallen for ten days.

"Everwho had to walk outta here'd be in trouble."

Glad for the sun and for the flashlight, I could imagine night lightning as it lit up thrashing branches and swung a volt-axe into a trunk. Only once an hour or so did we come upon high ground occupied by river "camps," the Southern version of "cottages." At one such place, two sixtyish men strolled together, country capped, and a down-home phrase wafted to us: "Them boys was . . ."

Like Huck Finn and Jim, my partner and I slipped freely on. As the air warmed, the swamp began to exude the pungency of growth and decay inseparable. Shirts were doffed, sun oil applied. Around another curve and the breeze cooled our faces and rilled the water. I tried to ignore the occasional sound of a light airplane or the contrail of a jet that obtruded as if into a carelessly made movie.

A woodpecker pock-pock-pocked, a deep frog-horn sounded, a bird shrieked. Others sounded raucous, some melancholy, one or two returned my call, and by noon we had heard side one of the Audubon record. Two lean ducks sped down the sky. From a green base of lily pads a pair of egrets took white wing.

Now the turtles, or "cooters," sunned themselves on logs and plopped into the water at our approach. Fish-shaped eruptions broke the water at random times. On the water's surface, skating bugs zigged and zagged. "A pilot!" The copperhead eluded our chase by wriggling its unlikely narrowness to shore.

"There's a fisherman."

"Must be gettin' near a landing." Our party stopped for lunch on the bank by a highway bridge. As a pair of fishermen called it quits and secured their boat to a truck, a pistol handle stuck out of one gent's overalls.

"Is that for snakes?"

"Yep."

After lunch all of our group embarked except for a fellow still dozing onshore in the shade of his red cap. We watched as his canoeing partner pulled away from shore, leaving him to doze. Laughing at this practical joke, my companion and I drew past the man's partner (also his son), took the lead, and pulled wood for an hour or so. Downriver we made out the shapes of two people who extended fishing poles from their boat. It was, strangely enough, a canoe. And the closer we approached, the more the fishermen, apparently father and son, resembled the pair we had left upriver split between bank and boat. Yet there was that red cap, and beneath it, the smile of the erstwhile dreamer.

Winding slowly, trancelike, I stirred from a reverie to number the cans of soda pop remaining in the cooler. A story came to mind that veterans had told that morning: on the last trip, anyone they had met along the way would declare, "It's about twelve miles ahead." The humor had faded now as we turned through the cypresses, the oaks, the maples, the gums, the river birches, the occasional longleaf pine, the unknown splashers.

Once more lifting the paddle to the other side, I muscled it through the dark water. Had we entered some twilight zone where the river would never end? Would we escape from our escape from civilization? "Twelve miles ahead." Turn, turn, twelve, twelve, another soda pop disappeared.

Nailed upon a tree trunk appeared a wooden arrow with the words "Dorman Realty." I treasured its letters and its sawed point. As the sun heated up, we glided past pots set out to mark fishing lines. Twelve miles. My butt was so sore I tried kneeling. We passed some rough-looking characters with long guns in their boat: "How far is it?" "Twelve miles, and if you was a deer I'd carry you back myself." This imagined exchange helped me speed around a couple more bends.

There on the left was the vision of a shirtless man who sat in a lawn chair and listened to a ball game on the radio of his car. On we hauled until a metal crowd of boats and pickups appeared.

At last I extended a tennis shoe into the cool water and carefully transferred my weight onto the cement ramp. Soon our roof-borne vessel sped upside down above us. With relief I watched the landscape of a county that barely rose between a wild river and a strip of motels, campground-cities, sea-walls, trucked-in palm trees, and miniature golf courses jammed with man-made dinosaurs, volcanoes, and giant mushrooms.

6

"Think It'll Stick?"

Low land and a high water table: these forced a person building a house to import dirt rather than excavate it. So one day many a dump truck clattered and boomed its load into the clearing in our woods, then deposited mounds of dirt to discourage rainwater from draining under the house. I had learned that "low" property like ours was prone to flood and slow to drain, and that basements were as rare as tumbleweeds in the Independent Republic of Horry.

But how can one *stay*, I asked myself uneasily, without a basement? I wanted to dig in, not to rest on the surface like the house trailers that were so common in the area. With new appreciation I recalled the basements in my hometown.

Not only did they fix our houses into the earth, but they afforded precious lawn space by putting storage and utility areas under the ground rather than atop it. I saw them, moreover, as havens from propriety, like the vacant lots. They had no carpeting or wallpaper but, instead, damp concrete, washing machines, clotheslines, and heating ducts. They offered a place for Indian Guides to play games, Cub Scouts to fashion a papier-mâché model or cut out a jigsaw puzzle, and teenagers to dance.

In this one, an A&P grocery cart served as a laundry basket; in that, some liquor bottles, half-hidden from a disapproving spouse, slowly emptied; in another, an old man puttered next to a cavelike foundation made of rocks. In our basement a model train circled a piece of plywood as it emitted an electrical smell. Equipment for making cherry wine from our trees was shelved near Great Grandma Capps's canning stove and near bottles of brown, homemade applesauce. Baskets of clinkers waited to be hauled out and a dense bag of water-softening salt to be poured in. Potatoes popped out eyes to see in the dim light.

Now, on Graham Road, I was relieved to see the carpenters at least dig footings down through the borrowed dirt and into the "gumbo" beneath. This type of clay, however, bothered me, because although it shattered shovels when dry, it became pudding when wet. But the work proceeded. On a wonderful. morning the concrete truck labored and slipped among the trees, then slid the blessed glue down the chute and into the molds. Steel reinforcement rods were added to counteract the gumbo's tendency to wrinkle a foundation. Then another truck delivered thousands of Old Charleston—style bricks. Shaped from a more reliable local clay, they began to compose the above-ground perimeter.

Often that summer I went out to the holy site. How gratifying, how strange, to poke around one's own house under construction, sniffing those lumber and chalky smells as I had done in my boyhood. The studs rose, framed by the "joices" (as pronounced by the carpenters from the Daisy community). At last it stood finished: American Home. Its plan ordered from a magazine, it was sort of a New England ranch house paneled outside by California redwood and circled by Carolina pines. It was certified "Horry County," however, by the cigarette burn on a marble wash basin.

With a nail I poked holes to plant tiny, expensive centipede grass seed, a variety that grows only as far north as

Raleigh, North Carolina. As a definition and barrier between the driveway and grass, I bought some railroad ties from a lumberyard. Our young neighbor, Chuck Purvis, helped me arrange them. Then I dug and wrestled to embed them.

~~~

When white flakes had begun to pirouette silently down from the gray onto Glen Ellyn, children had asked eagerly, "Think it'll stick?" Marge and I sometimes asked the same question about our attempt to settle. Yet we gradually felt more local — while at the same time sporting the sunglasses and camera of tourists.

"Snow!" I no longer exclaimed this to myself when glimpsing a white patch of sand near the college. But I relished living near the sand of the beach. Neither of us could believe it when a hose washed a residue of the seashore off our tanned selves and onto our own grass. Once we even walked a canoe through the breakers, paddled around in the ocean, and rode a wave ashore to a crash landing.

Marge had driven to the hospital innumerable times to deliver a baby or check on a patient. One night I accompanied her as far as the parking lot. There I sipped wine while the radio played music and, across Highway 501, the orange letters MOTOR INN burned on and off under the sky-blue word CONWAY and over the thick arrow of bulbs that kept shooting stroboscopically until raindrops on the windshield produced a mystical blur of blinks.

No longer did I stare at the prisoners who shoveled out our ditch under a watchful gaze and gun. I had learned to say "Grayum" Road instead of "Gram." And I had started getting used to directing longtime residents to our house by triangulation with those of our next-door neighbors, who were more locally grown.

I was trying to pronounce "palmetto" correctly: the name of the state's tree began like "pal," not "palm" (a species to which it bore a squat resemblance). I was on the verge of distinguishing among Lakeland, Lakeside, and Lakewood streets, and I had figured out that they all skirted Kingston Lake or one of its branches that almost reached the canal. At the Octopus, I rarely took Sherwood Drive instead of Long Avenue. And although the area's history seemed a rather thin soup, I was fascinated to learn at a scholarly conference that the word "bluff" was used by colonists of South Carolina to mean a riverbank with higher sides. From a storekeeper I also learned that two inches of water and two tablespoons of turpentine boiling on the stove keeps the flu from spreading: "That's what the preachers do when they visit the sick."

I had spent many a Friday hour with the Lions Club. There was John Jones, alighting from his bicycle after riding from his office in the old Langston house, a family and civic heirloom. I had heard dozens of Clemson-Carolina jokes. Lion Judge Floyd husbanded his wit for a few occasions. "Would you mind starting over again?" he asked a long-winded joke-teller. "I forgot the first part." The spring broom sale saw me peddling in a subdivision out near the college. There, one of the area's many retirees lived on one of its many golf courses. Talking incessantly, he seemed under house arrest.

"I moved to this place and they said I couldn't join the golf course."

"Maybe you could join a civic club."

"Oh, I've been in all of 'em up North—Kiwanis, Rotary . . ." He reminded me of a customer on my paper route who, shortly before his obituary appeared in the *Glen Ellyn News,* had stumped around his house on gray swollen legs and spoke to me in a sort of kindly panic about one thing after another.

At last I extricated myself with a new appreciation of my young potential to weave my lone straw into the social broom.

~~~

Our property continued to take form. For the driveway we ordered a load of coquina, a mass of whitish-gray shell fragments they used in the coastal area as a semipaving material. Finding the piles shovel-proof, I asked my neighbor, Mr. Sonny Long, if he would turn loose his tractor-and-blade upon it, and soon a firm surface stretched to the road.

The Lion Auditor helped me dig some extra border grass from his yard, and I planted it along the railroad ties. And one of the town's most venerable citizens, a retired teacher who had met Marge in a pottery class, encouraged us to dig up a few dogwoods from her arboretumlike property. Her place adjoined a stand of sky-poking cypresses. Next to them, on a pine, a fat serpent of a vine wound up, up, a hundred feet to its goal, a squirrel's nest. Miss Snider's childhood home rambled atop a true bluff on Kingston Lake. In the deep shade, within the two hundred linear feet of porches and under eleven-foot high wood-strip ceilings, hung local art as well as historical maps of river and town that she had helped produce. She tended to her wild birds, her heirlooms, and memories, as a kind of civic votaress. That is, when she wasn't pumping her blue bike around town or striding past students fifty years younger while on one of Joe Pinson's field trips.

A nurse at the hospital let us hack out a peach tree from the main mass of roots, but one day while I was giving a tour of our yard, my finger pointed proudly at a dead stick. As for the pines, large or small, I admired them and wondered why natives sometimes disparaged and even cut them.

I started to replace the plywood walk, splitting many a brick at an angle to compose the curve around the V-pine and to fan out the ends. With the house built, the trees seemed too crowded for their own good. So after painstakingly making choices, we called in Mr. John L. "Buck" Brown with his chain saw. This black man, sixtyish, looked no more prepossessing than his old red pickup with its white door. His teeth were a memory and his pant cuffs cascaded over his shoes. But how artfully his hand cajoled the trees so they slammed down where he wanted them. We enjoyed each other's company, and before long my title, "Mr. Boss Man," warmed to "Mr. Randall."

After this culling of the woods, the particulars could be seen more clearly. One day an entirely new tree presented itself; after much puzzlement over the manual, we concluded it was a "hackberry." By this time, wondering how we could have confused gums with maples, I nevertheless discovered a new species that seemed to be everywhere with its variegated bark—black, tan, and white. And those other attractive plants, were they trees or bushes? And what about these angular jobs?

On a second tour Joe Pinson informed us that the hackberry was a viburnum, and the other new species a black, or Tupelo, gum, unrelated to the sweet gum. The treelets were persimmons. For me such a fruit had been strictly literary, having to do with wrinkled or sour faces. Joe reminded me that the glossy bushes were gallberries, and he patiently corrected my notion that the vine (yellow jessamine) was part of the myrtle plant next to it. We learned that the angular bush was a ligustrum, or privet hedge. Our guide also pointed out Virginia creeper, a *Magnolia virginiana,* Japanese honeysuckle, two kinds of fern, dog fennel, sedge, wild cherry, elderberry, and several wildflowers: ironweed, partridge pea, bone set, pluchea, and meadow beauty.

~~~

One day our gradual home-making was shaken by some bad news. Our neighbor, young Chuck Purvis, had been killed. The wreck had happened where Lakeland made a sharp curve and where autumn always put an orange torch to a thick pyracantha bush. Now in the Purvises' carport the barbells had been replaced by potted flowers given in Chuck's memory. Each evening we turned onto our rutted street as if driving to a funeral.

As time went on, I occasionally recognized a name in the obituaries—of a colleague, a square dancer, a Lion, even a student. I would remember sad things about the only other place I had "stayed."

Glen Ellyn's staid appearance gave no hint of tribulations: the full martini but the empty mailbox; the unexplained weeping on the front steps; in a fabric-strewn living room, the armless mannequin that betokened the seamstress herself, once a housewife and now a hapless widow. On a single block, one child was alert but misshapen, a second handsome but retarded, and a third doomed by cancer (a word we eschewed).

As in all towns there were tragic misfits. One young fellow, who had hosted Scout meetings in his basement, once ran away to ride the elevated train around Chicago's Loop all night; eventually he confided his troubles to the gas stove.

From afar I could hear Glen Ellyn, like a stately bell, tolling out prosperity, propriety, security, and beauty—but sounding a faint, dissonant overtone.

In Conway, the unseasonable was becoming subdued by the recurrent. Pine needles covered the brick walk, and the Tupelo gum had already shed its last brown leaf when the maple next to it shot out its last red one. Autumn meant that we could open the windows again, the opposite of up North. On Friday nights the muted roar of the stock-car races reached us from across town. And all through the

weeknights came the noise of the hardwood mill (which I had stopped calling a factory), a continual hiss-s-s and an irregular CHUFF! BAM! SQUEE-E!

An occasional train would draw in from the dark upper end of Horry, crossing by crossing, different chords for different engines, somewhat philosophical-sounding for freights picking up lumber or wood chips. Sometimes an authoritative trumpeting in major thirds announced the Last Judgment; sometimes the *Lacrimae Rerum* would pull through, its blast a doleful minor sixth that faded broodingly.

7

Rhythms I

W here was the cold air that stings like a hurled apple? I had already made some adjustments to the Southern autumn in North Carolina and Mississippi. The calendar reads "September" but the weather repeats August; the body reaches for the flannel shirt but the temperature stalls in T-shirt. Of what use are old expressions like "Doesn't this brisk weather feel good?" or "When do you suppose we'll have our first frost?"

So in Conway I was able to notice little signs of fall. Sweat dried more quickly, the ocean water was cooler, the kudzu vine paused in its Asiatic imperialism, and the sunlight labored a bit to reach its wonted power—as if Persephone, in the middle of her luxuriant summer dance, had blanched slightly at the sound of Pluto's chariot. But still autumn brought little of the fiery clash between seasons. The warmblooded goddess just faded into an old maid. Many of the leaves, like duds in a fireworks display, turned brown with a *ffft* and dropped off.

In November the dog began to seek the sun, not the shade. The mosquito's stolen blood became sluggish. Pine needles obscured the line between yard and driveway. And smoke from a fireplace made the neighborhood aromatic, a special pleasure for a person raised where trees were strictly ornamental, heating fuel was cheap, and fireplaces were rare. But the old paradox lacked sharpness: that power to dispatch plants and quicken people, to redden both leaves and blood. In Conway, what looked brisk from inside—a cloudy October day with pine needles flurrying down—might feel smothering outside.

More and more this new Conwayite realized how in tune he had once felt with the daily, weekly, or yearly patterns of a town. A sense of loss, however, was outweighed by a growing appreciation, even a feeling of celebration.

~~~

The school day in Glen Ellyn typically began with a walk. Unlike in Conway, few students rode buses from the countryside or across dangerous highways. For the last two years of high school, Tom stopped by my house and I joined him for a brisk hike up and down Hawthorn Hill to another friend's house at Western. There she lifted the phonograph needle from *Oklahoma* or *My Fair Lady* and continued with us to meet another friend at the corner of Prairie, where he might be keeping the frozen air away by slapping his gloves together and doing a little dance. All four of us had a game of not stepping on sidewalk squares that bore imprints like "Laid by W. P. Conyers." Someone behind us would have been baffled to watch two pairs of pedestrians sashay around a square, no one missing a step or word. Through sun, rain, and snow we gave a wide berth to the sometimes invisible panel, laughing and robust. One more morning we crossed Main to meet the same hatted commuter strolling toward the station; then passed the house of Mr. Biester, principal of the high school; then continued downhill past Forest to Park; made a jog to Ellyn Place and began the steeper descent to the base of the high school.

After school one could stay for sports practice, walk to a friend's house, or maybe go to a part-time job. As a boy I might roam from a booth at Heintz's to the Studebaker showroom to the elevator in the gloomy Professional Arts Building, or to the window of the *Glen Ellyn News* office to watch the presses whirl, or to a gas station where Pez candy was sold (and where the drab uniform and grease rag of one of the proprietors almost concealed the swell of hips and chest).

At six o'clock the fire whistle blew twice to announce the civic dinner time. "Dinner" meant "supper," never the Southern "lunch," except for a fancy meal on Sunday. And supper was almost always eaten at home. A trip downtown to our single fast-food outlet, the little Prince Castle, was a luxury, and even there the lady prepared the hamburgers-to-go in an unhurried way.

Every Saturday afternoon, kids would pack the Glen Theatre across from the station on Crescent. There the rousing music of "News of the World" would drown out its own imminent demise, and one of the last to-be-continued cliffhangers might follow. Then Heidi might rise from her wheelchair, or the Incredible Man shrink, or King Solomon have his mine breached. Francis the Mule might talk or Harvey the Rabbit stay mum. Who ever noticed that an occasional Indian spoke with a New York accent? Afterwards, like Plato's cave dwellers, we would emerge to the painful sunlight of reality. Chrome bumpers glinted above silver gum wrappers or slush, while automobile horns sounded at random and perhaps a multiengine freight churned out smoke.

Saturday evening often brought a cocktail party for adults. In a town built on self-control and self-effacement, Dionysius, the god of revelry, was granted a one-night visa.

Church made its usual demands the next morning. Atheists were as rare as kivas, krewes, or kumquats. Partly because of the growing population, churches flourished, so a second Lutheran church was built, a new Christian Science sanctuary rose at Hawthorn and Main, and a modern Presbyterian sanctuary turned the old one next to it into a chapel. Stores still kept the Sabbath, except perhaps for Tauber's little grocery with its welcome lights on a winter evening. Sunday was indeed a day of family rest. Afternoons meant "Victory at Sea" or "Omnibus" on television, perhaps some chores, maybe a visit with relatives or a drive.

If television jeopardized the Saturday matinee, it rendered another communal affair defunct. The Sunday Evening Club had brought famous people to the handsome auditorium of Glenbard High School: Charles Laughton, Robert Merrill, Edward Everett Horton. A performance of Shaw's *Pygmalion* had displayed the Wells family's pair of china figurines in the background of one scene. After the middle '50s, the club's events were no more.

Like an alarm clock, the railroad bells started off Monday morning and the work week.

Every other Tuesday night in the junior high school years, at least a hundred of us would dress up and get a ride to a hall downtown, where we would learn the fox trot, the jitterbug, the waltz, and the cha-cha. Couples would whirl or toe-heel about, the whole group gradually circling counterclockwise while a few mothers beamed their approval beside the refreshment table.

On Wednesday afternoon the bank and most stores closed for a civic siesta in order to stay open on Saturday morning for the benefit of commuters, some of whom wore their old army fatigues. On Saturday afternoon in fall, many of the high school students and a number of adult boosters watched the football game down by Lake Ellyn. On weekend nights, dating couples would park by the lake to "watch the submarine races."

～～～

Our four seasons were as distinct as our four directions. In fact, pondering from the remove of decades, I discovered that my own image of the year's course resembled a compass. From January 1, due north, it circled through spring-west, summer-south, and autumn-east.

When the ivy turned crimson on the walls and buttresses of the high school, stalks in the small cornfield behind Mrs. Kramer's house magically became tied into upright bundles, and the Chicago *Tribune* again reprinted the comic-strip-style legend of John T. McCutcheon's called "Injun Summer," where the bound-up corn sheaves turned into teepees in the dusky smoke of an Indian village.

One afternoon in October Tom's dad flew us in his small plane over the town, which was almost obscured by white plumes that day. Even in Conway, just one toke of burning leaves, despite their hint of stale washcloth, would transport me to the burning leaf piles of my hometown. Before the piles were set afire, children might leap into their crackling cushions, hibernate briefly under their darkness, and emerge to pick off scratchy stems and particles.

Happy the child who could avoid putting up storm windows! A lovely free day was wasted as my family wrestled these winter-shields from under the front porch, then brought out the Bon Ami, the buckets, the hose, the ladder. Off came the screens, up went the cumbersome windows, now brilliantly reflecting autumn foliage, as my father pounded corners into corners and turned the fasteners. At last, bent-backed under the porch, we piled up the screens for the next summer.

67

Towards Halloween, children would begin painting store windows with colorful tempera. An owl-on-a-branch might be completed with gloved fingers as the afternoon sunlight disappeared like water down a drain. Few understood that our location in the extreme eastern part of the central time zone shortened the sun's already halfhearted visit in the afternoon. But we all sensed the need to tighten jackets and muster a little courage. Yet this annual darkening foretold a season when sunlight unimpeded by leaves would ricochet blindingly off snow and ice.

In the morning, Jack Frost had sometimes wrought his own intricate back-lit window painting. On the route to school, a child could get an instant of foot-freedom by sliding across an ice patch in a square of the sidewalk that had tipped or sunken a bit. Before Thanksgiving, white flakes usually materialized on the morning yard or in the air outside the classroom: "It's snowing!" went the loud whisper. As kids pushed a fattening ball over the ground to make a snowman, the torso wore patches made of half-rotten leaves. During a private moment, a boy could write his name in the snow with his own warm ink.

About the time Lake Ellyn froze over, pupils at Hawthorne School would line up and boot-slide down the icy walk, then sweep the snow off each other's leggings and coats with small brooms of variously colored handles. Children plunked backwards into the snow and flapped their arms to make wings, glad to be fallen angels save for the melting powder that reddened the neck. On Glenbard Hill, boots and sled runners packed trails among the oak trunks. On front porches, a hollow thunk! thunk! meant that guests were stamping snow from boots.

The cold could ache. A person selling Christmas trees for the YMCA might take his toes quickly back to the little hut, only to find that the coal stove shed light on them but not heat. Old Man Winter might even slick the train rails like a child waxing the runners of a sled. It was ice on the CA&E tracks (as I learned decades later) that caused the whole vault above to glimmer silently, a phenomenon that to me added to the mystery of the Christmas seasons. *

Downtown, snowflakes alighted on decorations, and shoppers walked down Main Street hill into a Christmas card. The Glen Theatre once again showed *Miracle on 34th Street* with a green-tinted filter. In grade schools, children pasted links of paper into chains to decorate the tree at home. (I once sawed off the bottom branches of our fir and sold them as garlands around the neighborhood.) In the high school the robed choir, carrying electric candles, proceeded down the aisle of the auditorium singing "O Come, All Ye Faithful."

Outside, to look upward was to feel winter's blade against the throat. To walk backward was the way to survive an especially biting wind. Toes were liabilities; unprotected outposts were called noses. Yet if one day the skeletons of trees stretched against a leaden sky, the next morning every twig and branch might be transfigured in sparkling white against frozen azure. A winter-upholstered youngster striding through the bright, biting air found the impulse to laugh resisted by an icy face. In the night-falling snow, a young couple, seemingly the only people outside, wandered through a dreamlike mixture of light and shadow, a black and white Oz that had replaced the winter-washed-out hues of Kansas. The snow obscured borders between street, sidewalk, and yard, absorbed the few sounds, erased all things tired or trashy, and, like a benevolent variation of the biblical flood, promised felicity for the young couple and the world.

Glen Ellyn's Story, p. 169.

Toward the glow of the street light, galoshes pounded down the icy sidewalk for that yet-unreached speed, soles flattening a little to gain maximum traction and balance: now for the last push, then the dive, and slam! Chest and viscera compress against the sled, and the eyes, half-closed to prevent freezing, pass inches from the blurry runway, the body helping to steer away from retaining wall or tree, absorbing each bump as the runners scuttle down the hill and up the slight rise to a stop. Then it's back toward the crest, panting to the rubbery jingle of boot buckles.

At Lake Ellyn, ice skate blades thunked down the pier's much cross-hatched planks onto the ice where young and old sped about, white breath pluming ahead, colored scarves bobbing behind. Speed skaters whipped themselves around the ice with rubber skate-guards in hand.

The magic, however, could fade quickly. Skaters waited out one thaw and then another as, on the roads, slush melted and froze down to the drab concrete that would grind sparks from sled-runners. A child walking along the road in tire tracks could kick a fender-turd made gray by exhaust smoke, or could jump atop it with both boots, or could heave it to watch it land as mush or stubbornly intact. Then for weeks the only snow might fly through town on the roofs of east-bound streamliners. Then once again a person could weigh snow with a shovel in gradations from sodden to airy, and perhaps jam a wrist when the blade cracked against the tipped edge of a sidewalk panel.

As winter dragged on, we endured certain days of raw grayness broken only by black, wet trees. It was best to stay inside, or to come home to Mom and the smell of cooking, maybe to wrap oneself quiltlike with the lamplit warmth of home while Sergeant Preston braved a howling snowstorm on the radio, maybe to watch Chicago's "Kukla, Fran and

Ollie" with its gentle humor crowned by Fran's nonplussed silences.

At last Easter returned. Its message drew powerful confirmation from the imminent defeat of winter. Lowly growths of fur, evidently a primitive form of vegetation that could live without benefit of chlorophyll, appeared on certain sticks, and finally our sacred bird returned again. The emblem of returning spring in the North: a robin with the twig of a pussy willow in its beak.

Vegetation once again gave off an invisible signal of life. Irises almost overcame a sniffer with their essence of spring. One Sunday as my family walked back from church, "Grandma" Allen down at the corner handed us a bouquet (and damaged the moment by reporting a bad word I had uttered). A newly cut lawn, which yesterday had shed a rich green scent, today might lie under a white message sent by the retreating winter. On the next evening, however, children could run around after supper and feel the sweat cool on the body like the invigorating slap on a newborn's bottom.

Near Memorial Day, children carried bunches of lilacs to school for distribution to hospitalized veterans. On our block, the white or lavender flowers were cut from bushes along Impey's Prairie, where they bent under cool rainwater and heavy fragrance. A parade to Forest Hill Cemetery, where a number of the graves belonged to Union troops, expressed the townspeople's regard for soldiers of the past.

Unlike earlier students, we classmates in the 1950s had no war to disrupt our lives. (Although the word "Korea" would forever sound like a curse to me, I was only twelve years old when the Chicago *Daily News* headline announced an armistice.) The newly printed scent of the high school yearbook, *The Pinnacle*, concluded an orderly sequence that had begun in kindergarten with the scent of manila drawing paper. At seventh grade, students from all four grade schools funneled into the junior high school; in high school, this group was joined by most of the Catholic kids as well as students from Lombard. Of the twenty-five smiling pupils in my fourth grade class photograph, sixteen graduated together from Glenbard High School.

At the graduation dance in eighth grade, girls could at last wear makeup in school. After the prom during my last two years in high school, a rented North Western train, with dance bands and soda pop, took couples slowly overnight from the Glen Ellyn depot to Lake Geneva, Wisconsin. It helped keep students from getting in wrecks or "in trouble."

The town held an elaborate parade on the Fourth of July. If not marching with the Boy Scouts, I watched in the big crowd at Hawthorn and Main as band after band passed, float after float, up the hill and down. Afterward the town enjoyed a picnic at the park near Lake Ellyn, whose water would reflect and then douse fireworks that night as we sat on blankets in the football field or on the high school ridge.

The next day, cinders once again flew through open train windows to speckle collars and newspapers. But for children, summer was long and lazy. The leaves shimmer-rustled as, down on the grass, their shadows sifted from dark brown to light and back to dark. The mourning dove sighed, the propeller plane snored across the blue. Occasional tires went lup-dup over the warm seams of tar that gave each street its own fingerprint, and that gently awoke children who had fallen asleep in the car on the way home from a trip. The great black tar cauldron bubbled out a mystical tune and aroma as laborers covered the winter-wandering cracks.

In the back yard a turtle that somebody had caught in the forest preserve scratched its tub. In the sandbox miniature towns slowly took shape and then rejoined the desert with the wave of a hand. Canasta cards wore out on front porches. On the long screened porch of 332 Cottage, we would sit in the wicker chairs with feet on the ledge, reading a book or listening to old 78 records. We might greet Mrs. Kramer as she marched stiffly up the hill with a bag of groceries. At night a porch sleeper would have to draw the awnings against the street light and the moist, cool air.

Summer also meant plenty of motion. The ubiquitous baseball-playing even included a slow-pitch game down by the lake that used a sluggish sixteen-inch softball. A racer my dad built us sped down Kenilworth Hill, while on the sidewalks, girls hopped between chalked squares drawn within concrete ones. Out of the basement came Boy Scout camping equipment. On the lawns, croquet balls socked together and Messrs Briggs & Stratton pulled my mower. Caddies got plenty of exercise at Glen Oak Country Club.

Like the movie theater, the public swimming pool was jammed with noisy kids, especially because few private pools existed in town. After a bike ride across the bumpy tracks and up the long hill to the far side, I would get a whiff of chlorine mixed with the scent of warm, mowed grass. In a minute I was arching from the high board, a swan in trunks, then racing through the water or flying in slow motion beneath it, then touching the drain at the deep end in solitary oblivion, then frolicking with buddies. "Can you touch here?" "Go under me!" "Try it backwards." Each increment of depth was painted on the concrete edge. We would scramble back up to the deck, where we knew just how fast to slap wet feet to concrete without incurring the lifeguard's whistle.

~~~

"I've got Mrs. Groom for second grade!" My new brown shoes skimmed over the yard to Mom, who smiled as she hung out another sheet on the line. Members of the high school cross-country team once again ran counterclockwise around and around Lake Ellyn. Soon the flames of autumn would sweep once more through the treetops to drop cinders and glowing coals on the grass below.

8

More Adventures in Not Moving

The day after Thanksgiving in Conway I ate a well-balanced breakfast of one piece mince pie and one piece pumpkin, then drove off into the country. The faintly green woods and washed-out brownish-yellow fields no doubt harbored many a plump creature. Although in my boyhood the only hunter I knew of had been Uncle George, I myself was now making a rendezvous with my hunting guide, Steve Robertson, editor of the local newspaper.

From Centenary, a name without a place, we drove to a remote farm, where he gave me a lesson in handling the borrowed shotgun. "Point it toward the woods, and you gently return the hammer to the safety posi—" The blast was so loud that I expected the trees to shatter like a window and crash to the ground as green and brown pieces. With ringing ears I heard myself say, "I guess the hammer has some tension on it." Then when I flicked back a release to recover the spent shell, it whizzed out at me, trailing smoke. "Forgot to tell you about that."

A little shooting practice made sure that a sweet potato would never fly again. Then we headed down the field abreast but at some width apart. Despite my success with the potato, I regarded my weapon apprehensively. "Concentrate," I kept telling myself; "If you flush a bird, release safety, aim, fire."

But how distracting it was to be followed down the rows by a portly hog—"Your friend," Robertson called it.

Nothing in the corn stubble, so we headed for the woods. Each of us sat in his own little nest for a long time hoping that a deer would stroll within range of a 7½ shell. But our patience was rewarded by nary a squirrel, only a falling leaf now and then. We did feel refreshed, however, as we returned to the edge of the field. As my guide was attending to his gun, it clicked for some reason—and an explosion of wings ambushed us. Although caught off guard, he still managed to fire at the same time I did because caution had put a "safety" on my reflexes. Anyway, we both missed. He all but threw his gun in the dirt. I yelled out, "Come back, doves, we were just kidding!" Discouraged, we ended up back near the pigs, tossing and shooting corncobs.

As evening approached, Robertson smelled ducks. After picking up his brother and a boat, he raced it down the Little Pee Dee as if driven by an instinct. We moored beneath an overhanging limb and waited.

"Duck!" Already vanished, it had looked like a pudgy arrow. The boat still rocked from the recoil.

Estimating that more sky could be seen from a nearby bank, I soon had one foot in the boat and another testing a root. With the vines shoved away and a different gun tossed ashore, I clambered up. Once there I surveyed the dimming clouds, then my little patch of land amid swamp, then that strange thing on the ground—a cowpie? But how . . . ? I realized it was coiled.

"What's wrong?" Robertson had heard my slow but fervent oath.

"It's a snake!"

"Shoot it!" I raised the barrel but to my dismay did not know how to work the thing. Feeling trapped on the bank, I attended to each step of the directions repeated to me. At last my shaking fingers produced the welcome BLAM!

In the pickup on the way out, there was some joshing about my derring-do. I began to feel qualms about the snake, which had probably been more torpid than treacherous. Nevertheless, I enjoyed bouncing along after an adventurous day.

"Look, guys, if we'd been depending on this hunt for food, I'd be a hero."

~~~

"This is the day we must walk over to the swamp and dig up a cypress sapling!"

Joe Pinson had pronounced winter the best season to transplant one, so off we went, although the moistness and mild temperature sent the hands of my seasonal clock whirring. In our leather boots — our foot-jeeps, our stride-hides — we marched down the muddy road through a fine spray. Marge sported a bright red poncho and carried a trowel; I wore my old raincoat and work gloves, carried an umbrella overhead and a shovel by my side. The dog straggled along with little of its usual gusto. Nobody was outside. Curtains were drawn. I burst into song: "O sing a song of swamp, O muddy-duddy-o! Come out with us and romp, O fuddy-duddy-o!"

Coming to a likely point of entry near the canal, we found that the wet ditch blocked us, so we backtracked to enter where the pines yielded to hardwoods. We hiked over dead leaves, avoided sticker bushes, and pushed through underbrush. The ground became soggy. It help a myriad of trees, many of them formidable, that stood leafless and tangled together, gray bark against gray sky. One trunk, about eighty feet high, stood out because it was white and denuded not only of leaves but of bark and even branches. Another dead trunk had fallen halfway to the ground; once tall, now long, it slanted across many vertical shafts. I was constantly surprised to behold this wintry scene yet feel no cold air.

"Look!" Marge was pointing to the ground. Brown cypress knees stuck out here and there. Then we spied the base of a large cypress, fan-shaped, at once graceful and monumental.

"There must be a sapling around here."

"Lookit, here's one!" My shovel began to slice the wet, black earth and cut a square hole that kept losing its shape. I had to sever a couple of roots that probably connected the plant to the overall system. Then I got down on hands and knees and began using a trowel around the long tap root so as to preserve it. Because the hole now filled with water, I had to work by feel to locate roots, pull them, and check the length of exposed tap root. Soon we coaxed out the sapling pretty much intact.

"Let's get another one," urged Marge, who had found a specimen about six feet tall. I enjoyed the feel of my new black knee patches as I walked over to it, crouched down, scooped out mud, pawed it out by hand, threw an occasional worm to the dog, tried carefully to isolate the taproot, asked Marge to bend the tree this way and that, shifted the trowel from one hand to another, shook mud off sodden gloves, and gladly got more on.

At last the test: we pulled together to feel the root yield inch by inch. "Look at this!" I exclaimed, holding the naked tree at arms' length. After congratulating ourselves we portioned out the various items and carried them home.

"Look at these!" we called out to a neighbor. He came to the door and regarded us but didn't say much. "Look at our cypress trees!" we prompted with arms stretched out.

"Those don't look like cypress to me." Marge and I stared at each other. We planted them anyway, now full of misgivings, rather tired and wet.

Joe later pronounced them ash trees. Still we relished our swamp trek, all the more so when we telephoned my parents in Glen Ellyn and learned that the temperature was two degrees above zero.

~~~

To chart areas for the Lions Club's spring broom sale, I studied a map of Conway and noticed that Graham Road pointed straight up and down. Knowing that it ran from east to west—from Sonny Long's house on the eastern corner to the old Graham house at the other end—I theorized that the cartographer had tilted the map to accommodate the town's elongated shape. But there in the corner the N arrow stood vertically as if giving me the finger.

I had imposed conception under direction. But how had my inner readout gone wrong? I remembered moving into the house and looking at the sun through a casement window that was partially opened and double glazed. Why was the sun, I had wondered, setting in that direction? I now surmised that I had actually been looking northward—but not through the glass, only at a western reflection on its surface. This mistake may have been enough to establish the false west. In any case, the house no longer faced the North Pole but Casablanca.

This disorientation brought more of the dizziness I feared. But with time, my interest roused at the notion that beyond the pasture, woods, swamps, Waccamaw River, and tracts of pine forest, the very land ended at sky meeting water.

"Want to walk to the beach?" At this question my brother, visiting from West Virginia, raised his head abruptly and asked with a wary grin if I was serious. No doubt I was influenced by that Saturday morning in high school when Tom had stopped by, asked "Want to walk to Chicago?" and, since I had to mow lawns, continued without me for twenty-two miles into the Loop.

Luckily the spring morning was cool as we strode off. In a knapsack we carried aspirin, Band-aids, candy, oranges, cookies, extra socks, Kleenex, loose change, and plastic ponchos. Near the original home of the pseudocypress we crossed the canal, then hiked down oak-canopied streets. A few acquaintances met our explanation with more amusement than belief.

Finally reaching the downtown area, we passed the Horry Drug Store and hailed my fellow Lion across the street, who was wielding a broom in front of his jewelry store.

"Come to the beach with us!"

"Come sweep with me!"

The clock on its tower proclaimed the time to be roughly a quarter after eight as we hiked toward to the old Waccamaw Bridge. Marked with a plaque reading "1937," it curved gracefully as it rose. From its crest we looked down upon the reflection of a sagging warehouse that backed up to the river; most of the other buildings, including a lumbermill and its smokestacks, had disappeared decades earlier. Ahead of us old Highway 501 stretched upon an earthen causeway toward its junction with Bypass 501. We gradually descended to level ground and walked along the shoulder under shiny dark clouds. A breeze rustled the sycamore leaves, cooled us, and helped dispel the fumes from vehicles, if not the noise.

"We're only about one-seventh of the way," Greg pointed out. He wanted to establish a "pace," a state which he spoke of in mystical tones. I looked back with mixed feelings at the receding bridge. After a half mile of plodding, I exclaimed, "There's the ocean!" Laughing, we continued next to a field that emitted a scent of pungent, weedy, boyhood exploring.

Shortly beyond Red Hill Chip and the sign reading "Myrtle Beach 12," one of us called out, "There's Oliver's!" We

were soon eating breakfast at a rough-hewn table while prop-
ping our bootless feet on the bench.

On the road again, we waited out a thunderstorm in a
warehouse and then reached the junction of Old 501 and
501 Bypass. Next to us on the wet pavement the westbound
tires went *sziz-z*. While Greg tried to reestablish his pace, I
noticed the bric-a-brac in our path: a turtle shell, a strip of
chrome, a dead snake, a pair of undies, beer cans. . . . These
all mingled with the wildflowers and butterflies.

We passed the miniature Travelers' Chapel and then the
crane factory. At one automobile dealer's I stopped in to get
a soft drink, then at the next to use the bathroom. These
detours provoked my brother to complain that "We haven't
yet gone three unbroken miles." I was more concerned about
unbroken boredom. For a while I computed the average number of vehicles that passed per hundred steps (seven); then I
tried to estimate the number of steps our trip would take.
Getting a little numb, I became oblivious to the staring
faces that sped past us. *Sziz, sziz-z, sziz-z.* A phrase came to
me: "Stamped by R. A. Wells."

Eventually we glimpsed the gigantic flag that waved over
an especially patriotic gas station. I felt awkard about stopping, but this time my stalwart companion never deigned to
look back as I made my purchase. Once more on the trail, I
chewed a hamburger, its taste alloyed by exhaust gases and
swamp stench.

"Camping World 5 Miles." This billboard introduced a
stretch so monotonous that a sense of progress depended on
a wristwatch. I also measured the way cookie by candy. At
last I found with relief that the big flag was no longer visible
behind us. A pair of wheeling jet fighters looked as if they
had been dispatched to salute us heroes, but then they seemed
to resemble circling vultures.

The instant Greg suggested a change of socks, we sprawled onto the grass, bantered, and let the breeze play through our naked toes. As we retied laces over swollen feet, Greg declared, "It's a pleasure to put the ol' boots on again." By the time we reached the sign "1000 Yards Ahead to Camping World," not only my feet but my legs and back were sending me urgent petitions. A thousand yards farther on, I awoke on the lounge carpet. Although the nap had allowed my leg muscles to catch fire, it had generally revived me. After two aspirins and a Mr. Pibb, I was off again, hailed as "Gimpy" by my companion.

From the bridge over the Intracoastal Waterway we could review the Waccamaw Brick Company, source of the foundation for my new house. When I wished out loud that something could help me forget about my aching lower portion, Greg suggested, "Beat you about the upper portion?"

The tedious pines gave way to a long, untidy strip of businesses. Finally reaching the terminus of Highway 501 at King's Highway, we entered a restaurant and shared a pitcher of beer. Then we set out again, rounded the corner by a Tilt-a-Whirl, then inhaled the stimulant of salty air. There before us white froth dashed itself noisily onto the shore.

With glee we labored through the dry sand, then sprinted down the firm, wet sand into the water. As we shook hands, beaming, a cool wave blessed our shins. Salt water eddied around the boots which only that morning had trod upon the centipede grass at 164 Graham Road—a house within walking distance of the beach.

9

Their Town

For all its swamps, Conway was bedrock in its culture. The place stood firmly upon the old verities of tribe and tradition. Marge and I, having strayed from similar values in our own upbringing, at times felt as if stranded and sitting on our luggage. "No one moves without sampling something of the immigrant's experience."* We often felt no more a part of the place than of the local telephone company —"your" cooperative, as the bill phrased it. We still suffered from a case of ambivalence. Perhaps there was symbolism in that fact that our house, although so excitingly located on the edge of the continent, was also on the edge of town.

Once when I telephoned city hall on business, the man declared, "You're not in da ceety." How could a town not know its own borders? So I had to phone around to convince policemen and firemen that our area had been annexed. At least one civil servant did keep abreast of my position: said the garbageman, as we chatted about sumptuary matters in the grocery store, "You like Scotch."

Why not move to the more lively beach areas? Because we wanted a place that would not be seasonally inundated by

*Oscar Handlin, *The Uprooted* (New York: Grossett & Dunlap, 1951), p. 6.

tourists and would be more cohesive. "I think I could leave Myrtle Beach now without a twinge," asserted one twenty-seven-year resident. Why? "It's strung out along the beach —and the people are too different." Nor did we feel much attracted to the quasi-town developments near the college with their high proportion of academics and retirees, and with their garages attached to spec houses so as to snag Northerners. We wanted to live "on the economy," as they say in the military.

"There's a 'simmon for every possum," declared an older member of the Lions Club. But was Conway the place for us?

~~~

The feminist movement had no more reached town than the glaciers. The male tended to go outside in nature with gun or reel, while the lady tended to go outside of nature with thick makeup and a decorative demeanor. Out in the country, especially, the husband was often his wife's father and son at once. He bossed her, was "good to her" if he didn't beat her, and even spoke for her when telephoning the doctor or midwife; yet on the other hand he was unable to wash his own clothes or make his own food. For men, civic clubs; for women, garden clubs (with the exception of one organization for businesswomen). The unpardonable sin was to be a Women's Libber.

Marge and I, by contrast, had slipped genders a bit. For example, Marge learned from an employee of the post office that she had the only subscription in town to *Ms.* magazine. Certainly I carried no pocket knife, even if I did visit an occasional tavern where the more combative residents tried to make news in the morning paper. One of my favorite natives of the area, from Cool Spring, told me a story with eyes twinkling in his sun-leathered face:

"A long time ago I went down to Charleston to find me a job. The feller said 'Where ya from?' I said 'Horry County.' He said 'Lemme see your Kabar.' I reached in my pocket and handed him my knife. 'At lease you're honest!' he said."

At the hardware store one day I saw the cashier smile grittily and set aside a bag of merchandise until the grumbling customer could produce more silver than that long blade.

The gun was not just a recreational tool but an icon. According to one local, "When most boys reach the age of ten years old, the father wants to go out and buy them a shotgun for Christmas." Dads taught sons how to aim, a neighbor boy picked off birds, and random blasts of a shotgun disturbed the neighborhood. Word had it that a neighbor had been kidnapped at gunpoint by a disgruntled house painter. Just before we arrived in town, one lowlife had shot and killed a game warden.

Another weapon was the match. Horry County had one of the highest arson rates in the nation. Cars, houses, forests, all burned for insurance money or revenge.

In this frontierlike environment, the beauty pageants helped to polarize the genders. In one activity, however, the boys were just as dollified as the girls. The annual Tom Thumb Wedding was officially a fund-raiser but more importantly a community ritual. In it, two ornately dressed children pretended to get married while numerous other young'uns attended them and many more adults looked on. The image suggested something out of the *National Geographic*: "These costumed tots in the Independent Republic of Horry confer prestige on their parents by being chosen to imitate a native wedding ceremony (facing page)."

As for the ritual of churchgoing, an unbeliever was a homosexual at the prom. Folks even attended extra services on

Sunday and Wednesday nights. Adults actually went to Sunday School, an activity I though of as childish. And I got tired of hearing religious programs on the radio. As I drove to work one autumn day after a hot summer, the air rushed past me like water in a mountain stream. "Enjoy it now," the preacher warned, "because there's no cool day in hell!"

One ritual that appealed to me, however, was the surprise housewarming. Natives who moved to a different house would find themselves the sudden hosts of a potluck supper. Marge and I, in contrast, were given a large cocktail party by her employers, a sign of status but not of indigenousness.

People also converged on the home of the newly deceased. I first observed this custom after an old man living near us on the river road took his boat out and disappeared under the wake of a houseboat. So one morning on Graham Road, I was shocked to see a bunch of cars parked by the farmer's house. I asked a neighbor what the problem was. "Mrs. Long," she replied, "is having a party." I felt relieved but silly. Another custom was to pull over by the roadside as a funeral cortege passed. The first time the car in front of me did this, I didn't understand; the second time I shook my head at such a display of sentimentality.

As for national holidays, things seemed a bit awry. I had first encountered the problematic Memorial Day in Tennessee, where some places closed and others remained open. But to hold school on that holiday! And in Conway, not a few businesses shut down for something called Confederate Memorial Day. Abe Lincoln's birthday, however, passed as uneventfully as my own the next day. When I heard an old-timer, Miss Florence Epps, refer to the "Confederate War of Independence," I barely kept a straight face. Of course after rubbing against three other Southern states, the sharp edge of surprise had been dulled a bit. Where I had once almost gasped to see the Confederate flag spread its **X** over a dormitory wall, I now merely felt indignant to see it fly over the state capitol. But not to celebrate Independence Day as a town? The Fourth of July came and went like the third, leaving me drum in hand.

Invited to view the Christmas parade, I remembered one in North Carolina—where the ROTC members shouldered their rifles, and the cheerleaders twirled their batons to "Little Town of Boom! Boom! Bethlehem"—and declined.

~~~

Blacks were confined to a caste and to a few parts of town. ("It's ironic," one resident pointed out, "that the poorest part of town has the best live oaks.") Many lived in public housing, others in ramshackle houses that looked a bit Third World. Two municipal pools neatly split the swimmers along color lines. Blacks had their own funeral homes. A private white academy dated from the time of integration, and at fund-raising time I refused to buy its racist and elitist candy bars. I felt uneasy to see grown black men maintaining the lawns of white people. Marge and I debated whether to "perpetuate the system" by hiring a black cleaning woman, even though the money could plump up her thin wallet.

I knew of only one black business in town. There, to my Caucasian eyes, the skin of the shoe repairman corresponded mystically with the tanned leather he worked. (Was he kidding when he returned from lunch carrying a waxed-paper packet and said "Pigtails"?) The Lions Club had no black member, unless you counted the cook. The monument to "*Our* Confederate Dead," by its apparently inclusive pronoun excluded a third of residents.

Nevertheless, this very chasm between races was a prominent feature of the town's cultural landscape. I felt like an explorer. At one point I might observe that the rift was deep, at another shallow, at another even bridged. I noticed, for example, that when workmen sat together in a truck, the white man always drove. But even some educated white people said "birfday" just like a speaker of black dialect. Although the churches were segregated, they were filled. One white person might speak fondly of being raised by a black woman in the days when people of even modest income could afford a full-time maid-cook-nanny; another might chuckle patronizingly about "niggers." There seemed an undercurrent of fear among the whites, yet there were no longer any black schools, so that the children of both races could, and did, misbehave together without visible harm.

For all its racial polarization, the town offered me an opportunity: living near black people was a long overdue experience.

In Glen Ellyn, just about the only blacks had been the white-uniformed porters glimpsed through the steamliner windows. Warren, however, was one of the handful of black residents. A friendly man who greeted me with "Yessir!", he worked at Patches' Hardware on Main. In its dimness he would slide the tall pole along the shelves to clamp an item and lower it, making his way slowly along the wooden floorboards as if walking under water. Sometimes I would pass him along the sidewalk as he returned to his quarters on Pennsylvania, his gait sometimes further relaxed by liquor.

There was a sprinkling of cleaning ladies. Willa, for example, was a wiry, petite woman of hard-to-determine age. "She works all day," worried my mother, "and then has to ride the bus all the way into the Loop and from there take the El to Sixty-third Street—she doesn't get home for two hours." Our high school enrolled fewer blacks than foreign exchange students, so we never had to deal with even so minor a challenge as a kinky hair among the occasional straight ones in the school washbasins. The only time I identified myself with the black race was when I played the "colored" Wise Man in a high school Christmas program. The most elegant girl in school applied the makeup: onto my forehead she rubbed the cool grease, onto my cheeks and nose, around my closed eyes, around and around, who cared what color it was, I would have turned Indian at her fingers, deeper and deeper, into the *stratum corneum* itself (the aptly named "horny layer").

~~~

"Did he say 'chicken bog'?" Marge and I looked at each other uncertainly. Yes, the president of the square-dance club had so spoken, and before long we understood the term to mean both a dish and an occasion. The food, a mixture of chicken, sausage, and rice, was often served at large gatherings, accompanied on the plate by slices of sweet potato — which to fulfill local dietary prescriptions had to remain unheated — and by iced tea, which had to be sweetened. We enjoyed mixing with all the people, including babies Marge had delivered or students I had taught. The dish itself even moved me to verse:

> Pluck off the feathers
> Throw 'em all away
> Take the naked fryer
> And simmer it all day
> With rice and spice
> And little hunks o' hog
> You get a swampy stew
> Called Chicken Bog.

Another appealing thing about the area's menu was the abundance of fresh vegetables that people bestowed on us from their gardens. The janitor at school even brought me a shopping bag full of collard greens, for us a lifetime supply. But we ourselves rarely prepared native dishes, eating them mainly at someone else's house or at a restaurant—like this composite one:

A plain building outside, with little or no foyer, its door opened onto a table and an acquaintance. The functional decor was little relieved by a few bland paintings or images of college mascots, among them a tiger prominently displayed. The TV might even chatter away unnoticed, just like home. A customer could order from among the following: hot fresh flounder (fried), barbecued ribs, shredded barbecue, beef stew, fried chicken, rice, potatoes, sweet potato soufflé, field peas, mustard greens that tasted as much of the pig as of the garden, salad, homemade biscuits, corn dodgers or hush puppies, tea (unsweetened available upon request), no beer, and hot, syrupy apple slices. Everything tasted good, although, or because, it was rather oiled, sugared, and gravied.

Horry County guzzled soda pop. Conway had not one but two bottling companies, Coca-Cola at one end and, at the other, Dr. Pepper and Pepsi-Cola ("Born in the Carolinas"). One carpentry crew even performed a ritual of immuring an empty Pepsi bottle on each job.

"They even put tea and Coke in baby bottles," said Marge. "No!"

"Well, for toddlers anyway. They go around sucking on the nipples."

Luckily for us would-be settlers, we had our own habit to support, namely, of experiencing new things. "Sure," I replied, when Joe Pinson offered us a perversion of peanuts accomplished by boiling them. The inauspiciously soggy shells were easily picked open to yield soft, salty, rich beans.

～～～

"Snug" was the word for family ties. Three sets of brothers lived in our neighborhood and at least two families held property next door for the children to build houses on. One couple we liked had grown up next door to each other and then moved across the street after their wedding. Marge and I, having subordinated family to mobility, looked askance at this tightness. We suspected that family-sufficiency had kept another couple from reciprocating after eating supper with us. To aggravate the situation, we had to depend on friends rather than relations, unlike the Hucks, Jordan, Rabon, Todd, and Johnson families that crowded the telephone book.

And of course "bedrock" meant political conservatism. One officer of the Chamber of Commerce thought it was a joke at first when I reported voting for George McGovern, then called to a friend in delight, "I've found a real live liberal!" I felt some glee of my own when I visited someone's beach house and ran across an old issue of *Plain Truth* magazine with a photograph of Richard Nixon on the cover.

The area resisted governmental activities like zoning, so that two trailers had sprouted near the end of Graham by the doctor's new mansion. Out in the county there was no house-to-house garbage collection, so one had to burn, bury, or carry it. Dumpsters added variety to the roadside with their maws wide open and choked with packing cartons, full plastic bags, and loose junk.

Adding to its conservative tenor, Conway and environs was full of military retirees. The gentleman who sold us our property, for example, had in his office a photograph of a bomber he had flown on numerous missions. Around the corner from us, a likeable retiree from the Navy had installed a mastlike flagpole in the front yard and trained an espalier to write "USN" on the house.

In what other state would The Citadel raise its walls, a state-supported military college? (Clemson itself had been a military school for many years.) Some wit joked that South Carolina was so flat because of all its military bases. However that may be, A-7 fighter jets from Myrtle Beach Air Force Base regularly zoomed over our house, and once a week a gigantic, dark plane (from Charleston Air Force Base, I supposed), would whine in a slow loop back southward while I eyed it like a chick in the hawk's shadow.

Luckily my allergy to all things military, contracted during the Vietnam War, had diminished. The process sped up when I began getting much of my income from the air base as an extension teacher. Through our jobs, moreover, Marge and I both enjoyed getting to know the airmen (a generic term for both male and female), many of whom lived off the base. Even various civilians like Mr. Purvis (Chuck's father) worked there. As a bonus to all this novelty, I encountered new terms like CHAMPAS (military medical insurance) and Hangar Queen (an airplane chronically in need of repair).

Much of the area's conservatism was familiar from my own upbringing in a Republican stronghold. So why, then, were these people Democrats? Members of the nascent Republican party must have started from conservative and turned right.

~~~

My allergy to tobacco, however, grew worse rather than better. Wryly I imagined erecting a sign at Galivants Ferry that read, "Entering Horry County: Unbuckle and Light Up." I could not believe the number of people that sucked in that poison with insouciance. As a volunteer for the American Cancer Society, I resented handing out the seven warning signals when the major one was a smoking body. To keep from challenging a tobacco spokeswoman who addressed my civic club, I had to bite my own tongue (dangerous for a Lion). As a state employee, supported mainly by taxes, I resented the smell of tobacco on my salary check. (Never too principled, thank goodness, I admit I still bummed a cigarette after a few drinks.)

Football? One couple in our neighborhood aimiably invited us to the high school football game. We were amazed to join not just the families of the players but the residents of the entire town. *Conway* was indeed playing. We found ourselves enjoying the contest and the crowd. But I had lost interest in spectator sports after our boys, the 1960 Hilltoppers, bounced their last basketball on the glossy gymnasium floor.

Partly because of bad run-ins with a couple of Clemson alumni, my prejudice raged. That school rubbed my fender like the bulge on a bicycle tire. I resembled a fanatic supporter of the University of South Carolina, Clemson's arch rival, who would bristle at the prospect of a Clemson graduate marrying into his clan. Perhaps I made that university a scapetiger for all that I considered jejune and jocky about the area. At one time or another we had Clemson graduates living on either side of us, while the banker across the street had Clemsonized bumpers, and various neighbors proclaimed their allegiance with decals bearing long-nailed paws, or belligerent slogans, or the secret runes "IPTAY." As for the latter, I once deigned to guess as far as "I Pay" but gave up and completed it with "To Annoy You." (The University of South Carolina offered its own solution on decals that read "I Plant Taters and Yams.") Another time Marge and I were strolling along the beach for a breather, when a lady appeared with a tiny tiger paw on the lens of her sunglasses.

From the middle of all these zealous fans—Tigers, Game-cocks, what-not—I looked back at my own five colleges. Certainly I felt gratitude toward them but no overriding loyalty, perhaps because my years were so divvied up among them. For a sense of identification with a place I found myself reaching back. Was not my true alma mater a town?

What should pop into memory but a trip to Orchestra Hall in Chicago. There I sat, indignant that not one person would applaud the playing that still echoed celestially—not my friend beside me, not his parents, not one person sitting in the orchestra section around us or in the heaven-scaling tiers above, not a single listener would cast aside timidity, conformity and pride, and dare to be first.

So I clapped.

A few concertgoers joined me, then more, then the entire hall, drawing a bow from the conductor and perhaps the rare encore later from the Minneapolis Symphony Orchestra. On the way back to Glen Ellyn, I was gently informed about the customary silence between movements of a symphony.

Was it I alone, now, who sat on his hands amid all the clapping alumni of Conway and South Carolina?

10

Islands

An aerial photograph of central Glen Ellyn, taken in 1906 by a camera suspended between kites, used to hang in Dr. Kenneth Hiatt's office. As a boy I would scrutinize it for recognizable landmarks in that homespun community of yesteryear.

Now I often felt as if I was peering down at my boyhood home from on high. From this comfortable remove I would search it intently, fondly. I could see how it was almost square, with two-mile-long sides. It was set apart from other towns by fields, a forest preserve, and a few new subdivisions where a scattering of houses on the treeless prairie had the air of pioneer settlements. I could even make out the formality of the town's cement gridwork of streets, curbs, and sidewalks. They seemed to correspond with its tightly channeled attitudes and behavior. Indeed, I came to the understanding that rivers like the Waccamaw and Little Pee Dee are not the only causes of insularity.

Glen Ellyn, I saw, was not a center like Conway, from which half a dozen highways radiated and into which surrounding folks came to market. To be sure, Glen Ellyn had a definite midpoint with its business section that, moreover, was literally a *down*town, sort of a topographical bottom. Yet the town itself was not a center but a satellite. Although living near the country, most of its residents made their living from the city.

One could drive a couple of miles to the Mullers' farm on North Avenue and buy stalk-fresh corn. A group of youngsters with a picnic lunch could see how far they could brush through the green rows before giving up at the sight of yet another westward reach, and turning back like discouraged mariners on the Sea of Sheaves. One night Tom and I even took his '49 Ford on a madcap rampage through the dry November stalks of some field near town.

But rural was foreign to us. We were likely to associate farm products with the city. Our livestock, for example, passed Chicago-ward through town at fifty miles an hour. The Cub Scouts or YMCA campers took a field trip to the Armour Company's slaughterhouse, and I visited the floor of the Chicago Board of Trade. I did see a rodeo—but in the Chicago Amphitheater near the stockyards, that vast termination for many a cow. Some families did own farmland but were absentee owners.

Not to overstate the case. My own Great Aunt Capps and her husband owned a farm near Elgin, where the Wells boys swung from a long rope onto the hay and ate pie on oilcloth. But these were really city people turned folks. Like Dick and Jane in the school primer, one of my walking companions had grandparents on a farm, but it was not until high school that I met another student who actually lived on one. Little did I expect to marry someone who used to ride a burro in the cotton.

There were a few rural signs in Glen Ellyn. A leaping, flapping rooster at the end of Main once sent me pedaling away from its beak and talons. When I was little, a blacksmith's shop even stood on Crescent Boulevard—an unfathomable mystery, because the only horses belonged to Mr. Goodrich, who also owned the only wagons aside from the bare-rimmed ones on the North Western platform. On Linden a rusty windmill could be glimpsed through a leaf screen as if through past years.

Near the cornfield that was tucked behind Mrs. Kramer's house stretched the rows of a large garden. It was close enough to the countryside that one day the gardener, while hoeing, perceived a shape of astonishing length and girth that slid among the vegetable plants. The old man, forehead sweating, used all his might to hack up this serpent which, in his wide and fierce eyes, had grown too big to be good.

For a time I helped my father plant rows of corn in the back of the vacant lot next to the Raffenspargers'. With some of those big yellow kernels I pressed "railroad tracks" into the mud by our basement entryway. But although residents sometimes pronounced the rain "good for the farmers," how many could we name? Mr. Rose, who as a boy on Western Avenue had taken care of a Holstein cow, now sold industrial advertisements for *Factory* magazine and gardened as an avocation.

Much more town than country, Glen Ellyn nevertheless offered more space and quiet than the city. There was a certain ease in lawns. They surrounded each house just as greenery surrounded most of the town. From next door came the metallic whirring of a push mower, Mr. Kranz having taken an early afternoon train home from the Kedzie Avenue station. Judy Raffensparger (now a widow), sunned on the grass with legs folded sideways, one hand supporting herself and the other ripping up pennywort.

Crime seemed absent. Doors typically stayed unlocked and commuters sometimes left keys in the ignition after parking by the station. (At lunch time a high school student could go for a jerky ride back and forth in the parking place.) A shoplifting jag of mine and my buddy's terminated under the watchful eye of his mother's acquaintance.

Almost no industry disturbed the tranquility. Where Park Boulevard met the tracks was a spooky brown house that manufactured knives (someone said) until an apartment building replaced it. The Ice Plant and the dairy still held out near the edge of town, but no neighborhood bars were allowed (and certainly not anything like the slot machine of Fox River Grove that spat out nickels). Just Mrs. Sharp's home nursery school at Linden and Kenilworth, across from Tom's house. Spacious and shipshape, the town fostered innocence. It protected us from the city's danger, diversity, and despotism (i.e., the Democratic political machine).

But by train, car, or chartered bus we could visit a museum, a professional baseball game, the annual auto show, a fancy restaurant, a theater showing a foreign movie. . . . Then we could recross the narrows and set foot safely on terra firma.

~~~

The town had no "other side of the tracks." Both south and north sides comprised established, well-maintained houses that ranged from modest to impressive, with only a few substandard ones. (If time had rendered a white-columned mansion obsolete, the new Biester Gymnasium actually replaced it.) When I asked why one house lacked a decent coat of paint, I learned that "The man likes to golf a lot" and felt indignant. Each house had a garage that was typically detached and built just wide enough for a car with running boards. Living rooms often displayed the conservative *Time* and *Reader's Digest*, perhaps volumes of the latter's condensed books. Nearly all my friends had a piano. Counterparts of the trees surrounding them, the houses anchored themselves into the ground and reached back by gradations into the previous century, picture window to gingerbread.

Tom and I mocked the lamp-in-the-picture-window conformity of a neighborhood near Chicago's Midway Airport. Indeed, there was snobbery in the town. "I'm not sure he belongs in Glen Ellyn," declared an older friend of mine, with a mixture of hauteur and accurate irony, about a clergyman with a passel of children and a hobby of playing jazz. "You can sit in the front seat," one person said to a cleaning woman, "but just don't get in the habit."

But a little snobbery is the price of good taste. "See this bowl that X gave me," said my friend's mother. "It's not exactly . . . what I would have chosen, but isn't it pretty?" I realized that its enameled fruits were either too abundant or too colorful. Among the town's unofficial ordinances: No homemade-looking houses; No plastic furniture covers; No toothpicks in public; No white socks in church; No slacks downtown (Ladies); No driving with arm resting on outside of car.

There existed a strict car decorum, so that one's automobile was a function of one's age, job, and neighborhood. A fourth hole in a Buick's fender was like a fourth star in the military. We reserved our greatest scorn for those black people on the South Side of Chicago who brazenly violated this correspondence and squeezed, by dark bunches, into luxury sedans that had been furred and flapped. One lady in Glen Ellyn did drive a pink Lincoln, but no one dared make a citizen's arrest. More than one family concealed the fact that their luxury car was secondhand.

Indeed there was a keen appreciation of a family's place in the middle-class hierarchy. When one mother had to work part time in a little vegetable-and-horseradish packing shop outside of town, it was a hush-hush affair, a social lapse.

Each of us knew what was expected of us. Going to church, although not assumed, was orthodox. During the ceremony, a stray "Amen" was as welcome as a belch. "A pink shirt in church?" another boy remarked to me critically, and I myself frowned upon the notion of a guitar service. Churches sponsored Scout troops, whose members saluted God and country, and wore military-style uniforms of the same army green as the corner mailboxes. Glen Ellyn subscribed wholeheartedly to one tenet of conservative philosophy: "The existence of a universal moral order sanctioned and supported by organized religion."*

"They're not from around here!" declared my mother as three women walked past our house sporting hair curlers. Walking more than a block was generally Mrs. Kramer's job, and curlers were private appliances. In grade school girls generally wore dresses unless the weather got cold enough to don trousers underneath. Only one girl of my acquaintance ever looked pregnant, and that was just before graduation from high school. Female teachers did not get pregnant; males smoked in the boiler room. Divorce? We were all Catholics on the matter. There were few stepparents or stepsiblings and certainly no "Mama's boyfriend." For the boys, taking off one's hat in the building was as important as learning the multiplication tables. My gentle first grade teacher ordered me back sternly: "Don't you ever walk in front of anyone again without saying 'Excuse me.'" Even our fight song in high school had a genteel climax: "Smiling to Victory."

*Clinton Rossiter, "Conservative," *International Encyclopedia of the Social Sciences*, vol. 3, ed. by David L. Sills (The Macmillan Company and the Free Press, 1968), p. 293.

~~~

That man cutting his grass in Bermuda shorts—isn't he
wearing business shoes? Indeed, emphasis on the private sec-
tor intensified the town's conservatism. Just about the only
government worker I knew was Benny the mailman. I never
knew a career soldier. One or two professors lived in town
but taught in Chicago or elsewhere. The typical businessmen, moreover, worked for a large company, and more often
than not in a middle-management position, whether in sales,
finance, manufacturing, transportation, energy, or merchan-
dising. Even professionals such as architects or dentists might
commute to the city. I always expected to work for a Company, and Tom even earned a degree in business before switch-
ing to biology and earning a Ph.D.

Although working hard, our fathers were not usually
"working men." Mr. Thomson did carry a black lunch box,
but not to the factory, rather to Argonne National Labora-
tories. As for labor unions, a resident heard little praise
—especially for a brand of featherbedding that allowed railroad firemen to stay aboard the new diesel engines. My
neighbor did serve as counsel for a union of, bless me, air-
line pilots.

All this business emphasis went hand-in-hand, or rather
shoulder-to-shoulder, with the Republican party. As one
clear sign, a morning paperboy might carry only a few
suspicious Chicago *Sun Times*es to a hundred cranky
*Tribune*s.

Such conservatism meant a high regard for industrious-
ness. It meant the Harrumph of the Haves. It meant enjoying the embrace of tradition. It meant an outlook that was
defensive rather than receptive. And it meant both independence and subordination. One parent hit on the exact image

for this last paradox by urging us to "Be an engine, not a caboose"—to excel, but along traditional lines.

The town was not politically charged. Of course sermons were never the place for topical concerns (especially liberal ones, perhaps, as Rev. Mr. Stevens must have fully appreciated on the way to Bangor, Maine). And youngsters were insulated from politics. Ours was to accept and to enjoy. Yet I cast my first straw vote for Dewey along with all the other first graders, and, as a college freshman, wore a black armband when Kennedy was elected. Like most natives, I had breathed in the communal expectations like the smoky autumn air.

~~~

As for ethnic features in Glen Ellyn—the word would have sounded alien. We certainly did not have the Bohemians of Fox River Grove, and we heard Spanish only when Desi Arnaz threw a tantrum on "I Love Lucy." I knew of no Jews. Long afterward I learned that two businessmen in town were Jewish, and one woman lived there as a presumed Gentile. Mr. Marx was a handyman who, despite his misshapen body, was always pleasant. Once I saw him hike his poor hump along the sidewalk and drove him home—to a shack half-hidden in a field outside of town. I was in high school before I met a Jew of my own age, through a meeting arranged by my cousin Joan. And it was to a synagogue in Oak Park that my Sunday School class took a field trip. "The first few years I worked in Chicago," confided a schoolmate later, "I thought Shapiro was an Italian name."

Although there was a generous sprinkling of atypical last names, these people acted no different from the majority. On my block the Polish were represented by a single family. They rented just long enough for the mother to run up the street, to where I was playing cowboys with her son, and declare in a thick accent, "No guns! We have had enough of them in the war!" Grandparents spoke like their grandchildren. An exception was Grandpa Spolander: when I collected for the *Daily Journal*, he once swore in mock gruffness, "I never heard of no *Daily Yoornal.*"

Indeed, the very pervasiveness of the town's British and Germanic stock made the variations more welcome. Thirty years afterward I learned that the black hair of Mrs. Groom had derived from Italy. The accent of my Cub Scoutmaster was Swedish, and the dairyman's European accent was essential to the Chocolate Milk Ceremony: he would ring the prescribed changes upon English as he opened the heavy door to the noise and steam, then handed us bottles of brown cream to swig on the curb.

But one could go for as long without hearing a foreign accent as without hearing an "ain't." These few cultural differences posed no more threat to the standard than did the scissors grinder. Once each summer he trundled his cart up the block to his bell's loud "Ding DING! Ding DING!" as if wandering in from some foreign country.

Unlike Conway, the town's deepest schism lay between Protestants and Catholics. "My Catholic friend," one child called her buddy. During the fifties, a Catholic visited a Protestant service as often as Pope Pius XII smiled. To some Protestants the Catholic church seemed highhanded: "If Monsignor Luke wants new steps for the church," declared my mother, "he just lays a tax on the parishioners." At dusk as my friend and I beheld the new sanctuary under construction on St. Petronelle's square block of church, school, convent, and rectory, the towering steeple, the whole looming cathedral seemed threateningly out of scale, as had the quarry-like excavation beneath it.

Perhaps you suspect that many of us were tuned to the

background music of station WASP. Later years would certainly reveal a wider range of channels to all residents in that parochial town. But were we not like musicians playing within the framework of one musical era, who never dreamed that its possibilities would seem confining in a later one?

~~~

"Those can't be shells!" I darted from the sidewalk to the little pile that distinguished itself from the rest of the newly graveled driveway. Hunkering down, I handled the treasure, then picked up a whorled cone and a few scalloped fans and sprinted the rest of the way home, racing back to load the whole pile into a paper bag. For years those shells, holding the sound of our town's only ocean, would turn up at 332 Cottage Avenue. Less exotic Midwestern treasures were the big quartz rocks that lined someone's garden; the robin's egg with its Easter-dye pigment; the hard, brown chestnuts that we shook from the Raffenspargers' tree and extricated from spiny pods then polished into mahogany gems; the "snow" that in summer lay beneath the north platform of the Ice Plant.

Although many fathers had traveled in the war, and my Scoutmaster, Mr. Dunning, bore a souvenir from Anzio Beach on his scalp, Glen Ellyn experienced a postwar stasis. I myself dated its start in 1945 or 1946, when a boy on a tricycle piped up, "My daddy's in London." The period ended in 1958 when the Munson brothers traveled with a Scout group to the world's fair in Brussels. Faraway vacations were so rare that travelers might show their slides of Western parks or Canadian provinces. Business transfers were few, typically with the industrial East.

"Randy! Come here! You have got to meet this girl." We rushed to where she lounged on her bike with a smile.

"Cookie, tell him — tell him your middle name!" "Culpeper." Utterly delighted laughter burst forth, because girls were supposed to have middle names like Jane and Lee.

Southern customs, such as naming females after families, were little known to us. Like China, the South was a place in a movie viewed from the floor of Hawthorne School's auditorium. I never met a classmate from the South until my junior year in high school. Although my neighbor, Mrs. Lowden, did speak with a Texas accent, some implied that it was artificially maintained, like bleached hair. The Rose family was the only one I know who drank Dr. Pepper, that Son of the South.

~~~

This physical detachment, this conservatism, this homogeneity, this stasis — all worked with the rhythms of the town to make the place a formidable redoubt.

How ironic that this very security could abet the dislocating changes resisted by a conservative culture. Upon this stable bank would be drawn many a traveler's check. With such a fortified base in his heart, one voyager would range as far as the Independent Republic of Horry.

11

The Child Is Bonder of the Man

From newcomers, a native.

She was born early on one frosty mornin' (one November mornin' anyway). Andrea was soon carried up our brick walk by her grandmother. In a week this offspring of one parent raised between skyscrapers and stalks, and another raised where "prairie" meant "desert," was bundled up for her first sight of the ocean.

As the months and years made their slow circle, Daughter helped Dad form his bond with the town. All around the place he took her, on foot, by bicycle, and by stroller. A baby, moreover, simply by virtue of its birth, confers citizenship upon the parent by a reverse *jus parentis*. As one woman confided half-jokingly, "With one child born in New Jersey, another in Connecticut, and another conceived in Texas, I don't feel all that close to Conway because I didn't have a baby there."

A baby is something held in common with a neighborhood. Mrs. McMillan would stop her car, get out, and hug Andrea, maybe play "peep-eye," the regional equivalent of "peek-a-boo." When someone fondly called her a little "feller," I thought one of us had heard wrong, but the second time I recognized a nugget of dialect. Mr. and Mrs. Sonny Long took a shine to her, as did their daughter Yvonne (the accent was on the first syllable). She baby-sat and sometimes favored her charge with bites of genuine Horry cooking. Andrea and I would now and then pay a visit with Mrs. Hucks, grandmother of the Purvis boy, to play in her living room, eat a goody, and light up old eyes. On the way back, the shadow of the child upon Daddy's shoulders bobbed against the light brown dirt of the road.

What should pass by our window one morning but a mule-drawn wagon! I carried Andrea behind it to a field near Mrs. Hucks's house, where we stared as a wiry old man yelled "Gee!" and "Haw!" as he grappled with a plow behind his equally dark antagonist.

With a toy wagon I would pull her to a bridge over the canal. We would drop rocks and watch over the rail as our shadows rippled in the muddy water. We might return with a butterfly wing, some moss, or a trumpet-shaped flower. Once I rode her on the bicycle seat through the Octopus to the Spires canteen, near Stilley's Mill and the Aberdeen curtain plant, where Yvonne's mother worked. Setting the kickstand next to a pickup with a front plate declaring "Jesus is the Answer," I carried her in to drink chocolate milk on a bench amid workers in coveralls.

Once when I carried her to the nearby pasture, we stood at the fence surveying the grass and the "horses' house." Suddenly the wind came up: weeds bent, trees whooshed, and a horse far down the pasture broke into a gallop, reaching us with heels clomping and nose snorting. Just then I glimpsed something small that whirled through the air. Closer and closer it wafted, and I recognized one of those biwinged seeds, the kind that had spun down so often from the maple trees in Glen Ellyn. Out went my hand—and snatched it in midair. My fingers unrolled slowly to reveal the object, which Andrea drew from my palm.

~~~

As the seasons came and went, the border grass obscured the railroad ties and a volunteer dogwood popped up from the imported soil. In our back yard, the magnolias were so "thrifty" (i.e., thriving) that I had to retransplant them to a cleaner space while Andrea and the new neighbor girl watched me wrestle wheelbarrow, plastic sheet, and root balls.

By the time we cut down trees that the forester had judged diseased or overcrowded, many an earlier stump had rotted enough for me to chop it out with considerable oomph. The remaining trunks had grown stouter. Perched on an extension ladder and holding aloft a far-extended saw borrowed from the forester, I had strained to prune many a dead pine branch. With our ample supply of home-grown firewood, the pile had shrunk only a little since the first October smoke had left the chimney. Our neighbor, the former gridiron star, chopped us a bundle of kindling as a literal housewarming present. It came from a special type of stump, he explained, and bore the outlandish name "fat lighter."

"Take a whiff," he urged. The fumes gave me a rush as if inhaled from a turpentine can in the basement of 332 Cottage.

One day I admired a glossy vine whose woody stem scaled a pine trunk. After counting leaf clusters, however, I whispered, "You don't suppose . . ." A thorough and apprehensive inspection led to a declaration of war. I donned rubber gloves and started poisoning, cutting, and ripping. I ended with a battle rash on my arm, but in control of the field.

Our gumbo alternately cracked and sloshed. The occasional rain ponds in the front and back woods had seeped into the earth and ditch, thence to the canal, river, and ocean. During a drought, however, a great forest fire between Conway and Myrtle Beach sprinkled the area with tiny, snowflakelike ashes that smelled chalky-sweet. Around that time I had to call the Clemson Extension agent to ask what might be shriveling and blackening the leaves on our holly tree. "Try watering it." Never thinking that a particular species could be so vulnerable, I let the hose dribble and watched the leaves spring back green and prickly. My gratitude to Clemson neutralized my annoyance at IPTAY.

Once I expressed by distaste for the local private academy while chatting in the grocery store. My acquaintance (the red-capped canoeist) had a more tolerant view. "It's a safety valve for people who don't like the public schools for one reason or another." At this idea came a pleasant sensation of growing tolerance. (Time must have been chuckling, for the public schools had a rigid cutoff date for entering kindergarten, so Andrea would open the door of the private academy —onto nothing more pernicious than a reminder of my old Hawthorne School.)

~~~

The sudden bass crooning of a cow sometimes furnished the leitmotif for a pastoral neighborhood. Grass on the other side of the woods was sown not for lawns but for livestock, and property was not mowed but tilled.

One summer morning Andrea and I followed her bare feet down Graham Road. She ran, got bit by a fire ant, imitated the sound of a rasping tree frog or locust, and got muddy from the ditch while gingerly touching the brown fuzzy tube atop a long-stemmed cattail.

Down the road a golf cart appeared with a spaniel crossing back and forth in front of it. The driver stopped and introduced himself as a member of the Long clan. Now

Daughter sat in my lap as the grass streamed beneath the cart. When we reached the pasture where I had mined manure and caught that seed, "Mr. Don" pointed out the cows. Daughter sat mum as we bumped through the shade, breaking the quiet of the woods only by the whir of our cart.

We passed Mr. Sonny Long as he bent over a row of vegetables. He stood to greet us and motioned toward his garden.

"Sorry I can't weed," I called out. "Bad hangnail."

"I'll *give* you some but I ain't gonna *pick* em." We laughed, waved, and continued on.

Now the cart crossed Long Avenue to the property of Mrs. Durant, nee Long. Don pointed out concentric circles in the pond. "Fish," repeated Andrea. And now we recrossed the secondary road to Mr. Kingston Long's property. The concrete driveway turned to dirt in front of an old tobacco barn, just as if going back through the decades. The barn sheltered an old wagon. Outside was a still-life painting by Andrew Wyeth: a wooden rowboat lay upside down, its convex bottom displaying a "mess o' onions" with fat bulbs and long tails.

The dirt track returned us to the trail along the pasture, which we followed to its end at the hardwood swamp. Our guide pointed out the bull among the cows, then turned the cart around and itemized a field, row by row: "Beans, butterbeans, collards, okra . . ."

~~~

The farm proper was owned by Don's cousin. Mr. Woodrow Long was a lanky retired mailman, gentle and friendly. By contrast he recalled Mr. Goodrich back in Glen Ellyn, a dour character who had owned the remnant of a farm on Linden. Hunched over the reins, he would take kids on hayrides or sleighrides, incongruous amid the glee, frowning as if bitter that his fields had come up houses.

Long's farm included several disconnected tracts. One of these was the pasture. Two others I would see each morning I pulled to a stop at Long Avenue. Ahead, the Club Road turned to sand and veered into the woods. To the left of this stretch lay a one-acre garden of flowers, vegetables, and fruit trees; to the right, past a buffer of trees, extended the third parcel. I never could grasp the latter's shape—maybe a fat boomerang? This parcel itself comprised a five-acre field with two pastures at the points farthest from the stop sign at Long and Club. Its farthest edge deeply scalloped its way along the woods.

Turning right in the direction of town, I would pass the vine-covered gate and sometimes glimpse wild roses along the fence, which had irregular, handmade posts. In the late afternoon I would curve back through the swamp and emerge next to the pasture on the right that widened like a funnel or cornucopia as it sloped up to the field. From across the rows could be seen a pair of small barns, narrow in the middle with pitched-roof sheds attached to each side. The left barn, of unpainted wood, held feed, although Mr. Long told me that in the old days people had tied up tobacco under the tin-roofed sheds and dried it in the barn proper. The building on the right was covered with red asphalt shingles and held cattle.

"The cow's crunching with depressed head surpasses any statue," wrote Whitman. The cattle usually stood in the pasture but sometimes in the field. A sculptured calf might stand perpendicular to its mother, sucking milk; or a mother might lick her calf. One winter afternoon the herd stood motionless except for white puffs that issued from their mouths, and one morning they stood steaming in the light. Occasionally a pair of animals would strike a pose that no city park would ever display. One

rotund cow resembled a globe with tan oceans and white continents.

The cattle occasionally ambulated in slow motion. Once a calf bolted away and raced with the wind, and another time —what's this, a cow galloping through the garden trailing a leash and outrunning its owner?

"I'd be glad to have you bring your little daughter to see feeding time." So that evening I carried her down the sandy road. The farmer appeared, striding toward us in his boots and swinging a bucket, finished with his feeding chores, but he readily turned back for us. At the barn he opened the top half of a rough-hewn door onto a large, staring head. I was somewhat taken aback that a calf could look so burly, while Andrea showed little enthusiasm for this animal or for the one next to it working oversized lips at a trough, or for the full-grown version behind them giving us the murky eye.

"These are like boy or girl cows," I explained, "and behind them is their mommy or daddy."

"Uncle," the farmer amended.

The declining sun came between the slats of the barn to make the calves' ears translucent and illuminate the tiny hairs that stuck out from them.

"See," I urged my subdued child, "this feed is like cereal." Powder covered the calf's muzzle. As the animal wrapped its thick tongue around its mouth and nose, the farmer remarked, "That's quite a napkin." I learned that the cereal was called milo.

After a while the two visitors said goodbye, then strolled across Long Avenue and around the corner to home.

12

Still More Adventures in Not Moving

The puddles on Graham Road reflected gray sodden byproducts of the hurricane season, which came around each autumn. But if cars could just get up and down the furrows, who cared when brown water splashed fenders?

Horry Country was crisscrossed by about twelve hundred miles of unpaved road. At best they solidly amalgamated dirt with coquina, but usually they vacillated between dust and mud. In dry weather the pedestrian wore a thin layer of road, while in wet he hauled clumps of it home on his shoes. It was the stuff of adventure as well as philosophy.

For one thing it was comparatively natural. The road went barefoot, so to speak. In close touch with the elements that nourished the weeds, native cane, wild roses, and trees that lined it, the dirt varied nature without obscuring it. Without maintenance the road would revert quickly: frogs would sport in its puddles, snakes curl through its grass, and pines sprout where tires had spun.

Such a road slowed a person down. Although driving from the pavement onto a washboard or mudslide could give someone the "high blood" (as the phrase went), it could also reduce one's pace. Whoa! Those bumps were a reminder that just so much could be squeezed from life, so many seconds from the wristwatch. Even the ruts had compensation. Carrying our daughter upon my shoulder, I would switch from one to the other as the original rut peeled off from our shadow like a siding glimpsed from a train window (a game I had played in the snow while trudging along automobile tracks).

The road lowered one's expectations about human effort, whether technological or political. Between the desire and the deed comes the slippage. For example, wanting to complain to the county's highway department, I unpropitiously found no listing in the phone book. "Try the prison farm," somebody suggested. But of course. Then I discovered that the road could be paved only if widened, and widened only on the city side, and only with the permission of the city, which owned the ditch with the pipe in it. At last a compromise was struck whereby the ditch was first dredged out and then filled back in, and afterwards a new ditch dug beside it.

After much spirited public expression, what should appear but an armada of heavy equipment that widened the road and laid a thick stratum of coquina atop it. "Such elegance!" we exclaimed happily. A few hours later, however, the clouds dropped their own contents, and vehicle after vehicle became another dumpling in the coquina soup. Mail delivery ceased. The roly-poly garbage truck skated ponderously along the surface and fell through. We recognized the edge of chaos.

One morning the sun came up to reveal a car abandoned in the soft new margin. This brand-new model, rather fancy and sleekly gray, had sunk to the middle of its wheels to resemble a vehicle knocked out in a war. And now an actual jeep truck, white star and all, negotiated the silent road, commandeered by the doctor to reach his work.

When the rain stopped, a road grader had to plow aside

the frosting from the original narrow roadway, undoing much of the county's work. For a week or so things remained uncertain. The newspaper still did not come, and the deliveryman reported that his attempt had cost him thirty dollars in towing. When the clouds opened again, I scrambled to save our car by maneuvering it back out onto pavement and then parking it at the Golf Club.

One evening, in stomps my wife, not having learned that to be a philosopher is "to be prepared against events" (Epictetus). "I'm home but the car is in the middle of the road!" I found myself hauling boards and shovels. The car reposed near the spot where I had helped out another automobile some months before, to be handed in return a grateful bunch of *Watchtowers*. For a while I sat in the car listening to the back wheels whine impotently. Then a few neighbors, from down at the house with the junked cars, rocked the vehicle onto the boards.

How to invite people to one's home without being able to promise firm earth? We had to relocate Andrea's first birthday party to the church, and one soiree ended with host and guests pushing out a mired automobile. Luckily the driver was a fishing enthusiast who carried waders, which he pulled on to toil in the ditch by flashlight like the Mad Clammer. Perhaps we should have been more apologetic about that contretemps, but we had lived on the road so long that our idea of a good host was one who provided boots.

~~~

Marge dared to ask, "Don't you think Andrea should see the Christmas parade?" Despite reservations, I agreed that the child should witness her town's major celebration. An hour before the parade's start, I drove to the store and saw people already milling along the route. A shopkeeper asked if I was going, and added that she'd gotten a substitute to work for her so she could go.

Soon Mom and Dad were cycling to the paved streets with baby strapped in her seat. Hearing drums and music, we pedaled faster in hopes of beating the parade to the Episcopal church corner and a rendezvous with friends. And there they sat, reviewing the parade from lounge chairs. Richard Lovelace's dark eyes and solemn expression augured some wit to come. Now surely that's not beer in those paper cups! After warm greetings, Andrea found herself carried off by a neighbor, and she never did know what was going on, especially when the Shriners roared in figure eights on their motorcycles.

And Dad? Each minute brought a new spectacle, now sacred, now temporal. A group of marchers or a float preceded a beauty queen representing a nearby town, or a clown romping among the onlookers. A workshop of elves, who busily sawed wood and made clothes, was followed by the Bethlehem stable under a large cross. An entry drew by that was sponsored by the private academy ("Wave!" I urged Andrea as our neighbor child passed). Queens, clubs, bands. . . . "One God for All" proclaimed a float that carried four young men in severe black cassocks.

Across the street I spotted more neighbors. Then as a car passed between us I recognized that pretty cheerleader as Terri Purvis, who heard my call above an energetic chant and waved back. After admiring a shiny antique automobile, I appreciated a float that was classic in its own way: drawn by a tractor, it was sponsored by a church named for a swamp.

A band passed: "How still we see thee lie, BOOM BOOM!"

At that moment arrived the royal progress of Miss Sun Fun, the greatest queen in the area. The young woman was stunning, she graced her mink stole—and she was my former

student! Lo: she waved in my direction, smiled celestially, and greeted me by name. Considerable razzing ensued from the onlookers.

After that, the parade waned. But then the tall red sleigh appeared in the distance. And now the round-cheeked rubicund saint himself is drawing near. Looking somewhat different from the green-tinted movie version, he waves down to all of us, naughty or nice. His beard almost seems artificial in its white luxuriance as he smiles, benevolent, jolly, and I wave back as urgently as a child.

~~~

According to Chaucer, April makes the sap rise and the people go on pilgrimages. One Saturday morning while thousands of tourists hastened to the beach, Marge and I felt the urge to hike to the Waccamaw River.

So we settled baby into a knapsack, stashed the camera and some bananas into a kit, and struck out. First we tromped through the multitude of light green leaves that already sprang from trees both native and transplanted. At the canal a cypress trunk rose high against clouds, fanning out only at the very top in black, rootlike limbs, and bearing new growth that was rust colored. A driver, jaded by the sight, merely zipped past, and another car went by with Mrs. McMillan's hand waving out the window. "Look!" called Marge, pointing to an exotic, pink-flowered bush in the woods: "Wild azalea!" Hearing her, a dog barked but kept its distance, perhaps lulled by the fragrant, balmy air.

Now strolling in a residential area, we admired the profusion of wisteria and azaleas—lavender, coral, pink, and red. Although the day was overcast, no Saturday morning cartoon could match the color. One azalea bush made me want to dive into it and drown in the pink petals. Dogwoods blazed white. "That one," declared my partner, "looks like it couldn't hold one more petal." As we chatted with some people working in their yard, I noticed that a blossom on a nearby twig waved like a white butterfly.

Our party reached Lakeland Avenue, a tunnel of newly leafing oak boughs and blossoms. God might have been speaking from one fiery azalea bush. By now, however, Andrea snoozed in her rumble seat, her gingham bonnet twisted sideways. Her parents snapped a photo here and there. As we came to the railroad crossing, I looked down the grassy roadbed and saw the track disappear around a curve in the woods. "Let's follow it!"

Crossing over an arm of Kingston Lake, we watched a man fish from a boat, his silent cast the only motion in the scene. At the disused Conway station we took a spur to the trestle that crossed the channel between Kingston Lake and the Waccamaw. Picking our way over its ties, with water visible beneath and beside, we halted at the midpoint. Somewhere nearby the area's first surveyors had barbecued a bear. And Kingston Township's first settlers must have set foot on one of these banks. Way down to the right rose the bluff behind Miss Snider's house. Closer to us was the rear of the fish market, and straight ahead stood Kingston Presbyterian Church. To our left the 1937 bridge ascended the Waccamaw, which flowed toward the next bridge at the Highway 501 Bypass, then toward our former cottage, then on toward its confluence with the already-joined Little and Great Pee Dee rivers.

Isolation, transportation, provision, recreation. . . . I searched the murky element below but found no sign. Suddenly an urge hit me. Like a native child, I craved the double freedom of plummeting through air and smashing into dark fluid. But before I could unstrap my papoose and take off my shoes, Marge prodded me off the trestle onto high ground.

13

Signs of Settling

O ur tap root, "along 'n along," did seem to be nearing
the water table.

I had outlasted numerous Lions who had moved away or
lost their roar. Lioness Rod's voice still lilted somewhere
between speaking and singing. Although the Lion Judge's
eyeglasses had gotten thicker, his wit needed no external
aids. "They say when you reach the Judge's age," declared
one rash Lion from the head table, "the second thing to go is
your hearing." "My hearing's fine," the venerable man reported
as he got to his feet, "it's your speaking that gives me trouble."

I had taught two or three hundred more students. These
included the son of Lion Goldfinch as well as his daughter-
in-law, niece of the Lion Chevrolet Dealer (himself the son of
Lion Judge). This young woman had given a speech on the
trousers-stealing Ghost of the Goldfinch house.

The summer breeze from Kingston Lake still poured down
the central hall of Evelyn Snider's house as it had since 1908,
perhaps airing out a few spirits. (You would not be mistaken if
you were to sense a resemblance between Miss Snider and a por-
trait in the Holliday house.) One winter afternoon Marge and
I rode bikes to Evelyn's place and found her sitting out front
in her orange Volkswagen reading the Sunday paper. "Don't
you like my solarium?" she laughed, blue eyes twinkling.

I had learned that the white McIvers pronounced the name "McEEver," and the black McIvers "McEYEver." Buck Brown's arm, the same color as the rust on his truck, waved out the window occasionally. Once I stopped by for a visit while he prepared dry weeds to make a soup for his ailing wife.

On the farm the cattle would make ever-varying compositions. One day they lined up in the distance, parallel to the road, a mural of black and flat shapes. Another time they lay in the rain with heads pressed to the ground like black and fuzzy lumps. When shadow darkened the pasture, a painter might have been inviting a comparison between the animals and the black stumps nearby. Cattle egrets often stood among the grazers: in an unlikely but eye-catching fellowship, white shone next to black, a slender neck-on-claws rose next to thick-hammed heft.

On many a rainy night, our car would try to skirt the luminescent frogs squatting on the Long Avenue causeway. A couple of times I had redirected a turtle venturing upon the road; one was a snapper—a snake-in-a-shell—that rewarded me with a hiss, a piddle, and a rip in the old sneakers I employed to carry it.

Once while walking at dusk, I jumped so abruptly that my glasses almost fell off. From a safe distance I beheld that dark tube, four or five feet long, stretched out immobile on the warm road. "Is it really alive?" I wondered. Tiptoeing around it while shining a flashlight, I counted the mouse shapes notched on its sides. Suddenly lunging backward upon itself, the fanged muscle wriggled into the swamp.

Around the neighborhood, a bird would sprinkle off bits of sky. Mr. Bluebird had been seen during my youth only in the Glen Theatre, where he had fluttered through *Song of the South*. A pair of crow-sized pileated woodpeckers would sweep among the trees and cackle maniacally. After learning that this species was skittish about living near human beings, I counted myself lucky each time I spotted the oversized birds. I remembered how a Northerner could feel almost blessed to see a red male cardinal hopping on the snow.

Although bees had taken over the bluebird house sent by Beth from Connecticut, a sparrow had nested in the hanging plant on the front porch (or a Carolina wren if you believe Joe Pinson). Moss outlined the bricks of our sidewalk. In back of the house the two magnolias stuck shiny leaves into my face.

One literal indication of settling was a small gap between molding and ceiling in the kitchen.

"Of a Monday morning" I would pick up Vivian, our housekeeper, next to the oak trunk that narrowed the street by her little house. On the way to our vacuum cleaner and ironing board, she would trade news, maybe comment on the beauty of the farm, ask about my family, or perhaps talk about her daughter in Philadelphia. Black emigrants from South Carolina, I was intrigued to learn, typically made their way there or to the New York City area, instead of to Chicago.

As a wristwatch-checker, I had been intrigued by the chair-rocking ceremony of conversation favored in the area. The white menfolk, for example, could slip into an intimate, genial kind of small talk that resembled a game to see who could speak longest without using a consonant.

I took a slightly painful step toward acculturation while visiting Charleston, South Carolina:

As I tried on a pair of army surplus boots, the black clerk continued to chat amiably with me and Marge. The three of us relaxed in the slightly dim corner as if in a refuge.

"While I unlace these," I suddenly remarked with bright efficiency, "you could make out the ticket."

"Oh, sure!" the clerk responded, as if he had forgotten something important. The spell was broken. He strode to the cash register and I felt brittle, Northern.

~~~

Every few months a southwesterly stink reached Conway from the paper mill in Georgetown and reminded me that many people in the area used trees as shade from the hot sun of poverty.

Although the logging practice known as clearcutting turned acreage into wreckage here and there in Horry County, the air was fresh enough to make a city dweller cough. Often Marge and I pedaled through the countryside, and once, her cheeks rosy and her sunglasses slipping partway down her nose, she returned from a solo ride to exclaim, "I went all the way to Maple Church!" Sometimes we would even make a full circuit, coming back past Blue Savannah Church and the yard with a bathtub planter.

Although I had figured out the meaning of Savannah Bluff, I was still on the lookout for a hump at Red Hill.

As we drove on Highway 544 from the Bypass toward the southern beach, gates would lower across the road with red lights blinking and bells clanging — to announce a boat. Its mast would glide by on the Intracoastal Waterway. Then the antique turntable bridge would close the watery gap, and traffic would finally get moving again. At the beach, Andrea could play in sand without having to remove fallen apples first, as her father had done in his backyard. Pelicans skimmed the water, trying to touch belly to shadow. I myself even caught a little flounder that dragged up the sand as if ashamed.

The family had returned along the Old Highway 501 causeway so many times, past the Lions Club emblem and toward the First Baptist steeple, that I had even ceased wondering why the sign in front of the Four Oaks Motel pictured two palm trees.

The darkness of the black-water rivers, I had read, was caused by the abundant plant material that lined and overhung them. On the Waccamaw I had ridden in Robertson's boat when it lost its steering and ran aground upon cypress knees, BUMPACLUNK-CLUNK. And one time, as several families had swum near the bank, Robertson's wife suddenly plunged out into the opaque water and brought up a child who, unnoticed, had lost her footing and gained too much freedom.

~~~

By this time I realized that the long-distance number listed for that courthouse office was for the residents of Loris, a village in the northern part of the county.

Against the courthouse I had leaned my bicycle a dozen times before walking upstairs to serve on the county's grand jury. A variety of citizens picked at random from the pool of voters, we had breathed in fumes from the Independent Republic's official vegetable, tobacco, while sitting in judgment on many a marijuana smoker. We had met one of the "Fightin' Johnsons," a clan based near the Little Pee Dee; his overalls held enough pockets for every grudge. We had also followed the case of otherwise normal men charged with using public equipment to construct what else but a duck blind. In the jail's kitchen we had eaten heavy local "dinners."

Marge and I had voted several times for local, county, and state candidates. We enjoyed the custom of greeting fellow residents at a primary school, of handing our registration card to Farmer Long, perhaps, or letting Andrea put the ballot into the slot.

On Hunting and Fishing Day we had looked up at the snout of a seven-foot, 490-pound black bear that was stuffed after colliding with a vehicle on Highway 501 between Conway and Myrtle Beach. On the Fourth of July, Robertson's newspaper now sponsored Fourth of July festivities—who knows, an event perhaps sparked by the grumbling of one newcomer. I had entered the patriotic speech contest and Marge had even served as a judge for a beauty contest. (Somebody's mother swore revenge if such-and-such candidate won again.)

I had felt comfortable enough to enter a civic controversy, not just on one side but both. Should the new hospital be located out of the city limits near the college? I hated for the institution to disappear from Conway proper and thus diminish the town's integrity as a center. Such resistance was shared by editor Robertson, the mayor, and thousands of the old guard in Conway and westward toward Galivants Ferry. But slowly I became convinced that the proposed location would allow plenty of room, draw patients from the fast-growing beach area, and avoid jeopardizing the long-sought permission of the state. During that time of conflict I paid a bit for my insight into a community that tolerated—no, cherished—the small, the old, and the local.

The new hospital did finally rise amid scrub pine and leave the old building empty beneath obsolete oaks. Around their trunks Andrea and I would play hide-and-seek while waiting for Mom, whose office was now separated from the delivery room by river and swamps.

The physician at the end of Graham had moved to Charleston after working so hard on behalf of the hospital. According to rumor (Conway's auxiliary telephone system), his wife had not been smitten by the town. As one neighbor put it in an artistically neutral tone, "Little Conway isn't for everyone." So no more oyster-shuckin' parties, no beautiful neighbor to talk with, no genial "Doctor Dan" to see waving as he passed, no more borrowed axe returned with a newly sharpened edge, and no more house calls for Andrea, the last I had seen since Dr. Hiatt back in Glen Ellyn had felt my appendix and reserved the operating room.

~~~

At the courthouse I studied a plaque dedicated to the French Huguenot Peter Horry. He was born not in 1843 but in 1743. How impressive to live in an area whose white settlers dated back to the Revolutionary War—during which Peter Horry himself served as a general. Indeed, when the two beach-hikers had crossed King's Highway at the end of Highway 501, we had figuratively crossed trails with President George Washington, who once traveled on horseback down the coast.

In a ceremony at the old city hall, members of a long-time family donated a pocket watch to the town. Afterwards I stood in fascination before this heirloom looking at the name printed around the dial, one letter for every hour: ROBERT CONWAY. The original owner had come to the area from Charleston sometime before 1790. And now this relic no longer kept time, yet preserved it.

Under the pressure of changes that were so obviously affecting the area, citizens now felt a growing interest in local history. The area, one learned, had earlier relied even more upon forest products. Pitch, tar, and lumber had been exported to construct ships. Turpentine had been tapped from great pines. And of extra significance to me, a locomotive had once chugged right down Main Street hauling logs to barge and mill.

Such interest, I remembered, had been faint in Glen Ellyn.

For one reason, the nation had been pulled out of the depression only by a tank, so history was much less appealing than the future. (In the attic of the high school art room, a bucktooth Jap leaped out at me from a dusty poster that promoted a scrap-metal drive.) Many did know, from reading *The Story of an Old Town, Glen Ellyn,* by Ada Douglas Harmon (1928), that the house and barn near the forest preserve had probably been a station on the Underground Railroad. Some knew that Mr. Biester had served as principal of the high school when it began in 1918 on the third floor of the

DuPage Trust Building. But who realized, for example, that a Dr. Frank Johnson had planted many of the village trees? History lay beneath us as unrecognized as the glacial moraine that raised the high school so far above Lake Ellyn.

By now, names of old Conway houses had slipped into my vocabulary. There was the Stalvey house with its arboreal air-conditioning; the Goldfinch house with its mysteriously swinging chandeliers; the Spivey house with its lawn sweeping down to Kingston Lake; the Holliday house with its four columns so massive that this passerby was tempted to try encircling one with his arms. The Pinson house was a sort of cottage dating from the 1850s, its kitchen originally separate.

One of the Burroughs mansions looked as if designed for Queen Victoria. (Don't let the pickup truck fool you.) To be sure, royalty existed in Conway. This difference from the social structure of Glen Ellyn intrigued me, for although we had numbered prominent citizens among us, they differed only by degree. Royal blood seemed a difference in kind. Although Mr. Biester reigned over Glenbard High School, with its castlelike architecture, he did not establish a royal line, unlike Mr. E. Craig Wall, Sr., of Lakeland Drive and the Canal Wood Empire. This gentleman's regal height was matched by his acumen in business. "If Mr. Wall dies," one man vowed, "I'm going to die too, 'cause I know it's the thing to do." The eminence of these Conway families ultimately came from a source almost unheard of in my hometown: land. Money really did grown on its trees; tobacco leaves broadened over its sandy soil; and tourism steadily drove up its value.

Across the alley from the Horry Drug Store stood the deceptively narrow headquarters of Burroughs & Collins, an enterprise that included farming, real estate, and timber, and that owned controlling interest in a prominent outfit called Myrtle Beach Farms. The one-story brick structure called to mind a bank in a silent film, with its windows divided into four large panes, set into fanning brick arches, and screened austerely by Venetian blinds. According to the founder's grandaughter, Mrs. Virginia Marshall, when F. G. Burroughs arrived in Conway, he put food in his mouth by constructing a gallows. Although his naval stores business was interrupted by the Civil War, he survived prison camp in Chicago and made his way back to Horry County, where he recovered the resin and turpentine he had concealed in the swamps. These supplies he floated down the Waccamaw River on a flat barge. In Georgetown, the point of shipment to New York City, he reluctantly bought insurance on the load. The ship was never heard from again, and the insurance money launched his business. Later it was Burroughs who inaugurated a steamboat line to get naval stores from Conway to the harbor at Georgetown.

Another family in Conway held royal status by virtue of Dr. Cathcart Smith's decades as a physician, and as the first specialist in Horry County. His daughter, Rebecca Lovelace, reported some people would weep with gratitude when hearing her father's name.

It was her husband, though, who had brought her back home. As she told us with her own combination of droll and drawl: "I never expected to come back to Conway, of all places, but Richard was really taken by it. He liked the idea of a hometown, I guess. Little things—for example, when the lady at Nye's Drug Store said 'Shall I charge it, Rebecca?'"

As for family ties in general, Marge and I had begun to regard their tightness more favorably. Were we not seeing a way of squeezing more from life that was the contrary of our atomistic, mobile extreme?

I would now pull over respectfully for funeral processions. (Later I would be a little disappointed to hear that I was simply obeying the law.) Marge and I had even purchased an urn niche in the new mortuary out by the college. Natives, however, regarded cremation as pagan, so they generally favored a roomier berth in the adjoining cemetery. Marge called us "nitchies."

～～～

Attending amateur plays had become my favorite ritual. The "Theatre of the Republic" owed its existence partly to another institution, Miss Florence Epps. A former speech teacher, she sometimes embellished her outfit with a scarf, and someone said that she once wore a dress with little mirrors on the back. She had lived in New York City. There were shreds of a story about returning with a fiance, about a sister, about sharing a property line but not words. White of hair graceful of carriage, carefully elegant in elocution, she gave an address at the ceremony marking the donation of Robert Conway's watch—herself treasured partly for her somewhat erratic ticking.

Onstage in the auditorium of the seventy-year-old Burroughs School, mean, dirty Jud in *Oklahoma* had just sold me washers in his father's museum of a lumberyard. Oliver's dad was a professor and belonged to the Lions Club. One singer was a client of Marge's, the mime in *The Fantasticks* was my plow-pushing student, and Dorothy of Oz was a lifeguard at the Golf Club pool.

By this time I had appreciated another way that a town like Conway differs from a suburb, because its residents have both business and social connections. "Hi, Margie!" pregnant women would exclaim in the grocery store. Even my barber-lady was her client, whereas my father's barber worked in Chicago. We allemanded left with the manager of Marge's office and danced at the Top of the Breakers in Myrtle Beach with Robertson and Cheryl. Our colleagues visited easily from across town, with no long drives back to the city. This double connection helped to weave us into the place warp by woof.

14

"What Church Do You Go To?"

My own habit of churchgoing, like a piece of luggage forgotten on the train platform, had been left behind when I transferred to a second college. As the dining car had sped through the snow-and-stubble farmland of Indiana toward Chicago, I ceremoniously poured coffee and returned the silver pot to the linen tablecloth—never guessing that my final transfer, ten years later, would leave me outside the kirk. For Conway (as my Baha'i acquaintance declared in good-natured wonderment) was a church-based civilization.

So when the Lion Chaplain said the blessing, I listened with respect rather than reverence. And although I sang "He's got the whole world in his hands" with gusto, I had my doubts. Where was the Great Scoutmaster of All Scouts? At home I might play hymns like "The Spacious Firmament on High," but "down low" served just as well. For in the universe there were no directions, in space there was no east or west—and a twinge of that old vertigo would hit me.

A neighbor on Kenilworth, Mrs. Clark, used to have a long sign on her mantel that declared something like: "God is everywhere, therefore everywhere is my home." But I enjoyed little such faith. Wistfully I remembered singing "This Is My Father's World" in Sunday School, and learning "O Little

Town of Bethlehem" while sitting cross-legged on the tiles of the grade school auditorium. But without the benevolent rod of custom that helped keep Horryites in the flock, this settler would remain free, resentful, and a bit envious.

To raise the stakes: since the next world was in doubt, had I already reached my Celestial City, where one of the windows at Main and Third had become a plywood panel?

~~~

How to *stay* in a region where an obituary added that the two-day-old "was a Baptist"? Where in Florence, the bloody hands of Jesus were nailed to a billboard? Where businesses witnessed with more fervor than taste: "Red's—God Loves You—Used Cars," or "Jesus is the Way—Ice Cold Watermelons, 3 for $1," or "Jesus Saves—Tires Balanced"? Where the cornmeal package thanked "GOD for YOU— Our Customers"?

In Conway our child came back from day care in a private home singing "I wish I had a little red box / To put my Devil in" and then asked why Jesus makes the sun come out to sweat us. Our friend's illness was interpreted by her neighbor as the Devil at work. One black church owned a bus named Jesus. A circular that advertised a traveling preacher invited people to "enjoy 22 completely different topics," among them "Goodbye, planet earth." Another "witness" visited a church in the country with his program called "Judo and Karate for Christ." According to the handbill, he would "BREAK 16 inches of concrete with elbow and 300 pounds of ice with hand. CUT potato off someone's neck and watermelon off someone's stomach while blindfolded with Samurai sword. LAY on bed of nails while 50 pounds of concrete slabs are broken off his stomach with sledge hammer. EXECUTE Kung Fu and Karate maneuvers."

This last testifier, I had to concede, worked squarely within what might be called the "Judo-Christian" tradition. After all, God commanded Moses, "Thou shalt smite the rock" (Exodus 17:6). And Samson, in an exhibition to end all exhibitions, "Took hold of the two middle pillars upon which the house stood. . . . And he bowed himself with all his might; and the house fell upon the lords, and upon all the people that were therein" (Judges 16:29–30). And the Psalmist knew karate: "Yea, mine own familiar friend . . . hath lifted up his heel against me" (41:8). As for watermelons, God himself smote Jonah's gourd (Jonah 4:7). God even "casteth forth his ice like morsels" (Psalm 147:17).

But all this heavy religious gravy made me dyspeptic. How to call a place "home" where a hardware store carried nine types of religious signs for automobiles, like "Meet Me in Church"? (The revolving shelf was capped by the sign "Conway Tigers.") Where at least one grade school displayed a picture of Jesus in the cafeteria, and the high school held devotions over the public address system?

Woe to the politician without a pew. To get elected was first to have church credentials. Prayer began the meetings of the County Council, of the grand jury, even of the Golf Club stockholders. When nobody said the blessing at an American Cancer Society banquet, I thought, "Well, the restaurant is just over the county line," but the oversight was corrected afterward with a benediction as a bonus. Public prayers, moreover, were sent "in Jesus' name," even though an occasional Jew might pay taxes or even be present. I envisioned another allegorical statue for Brookgreen Gardens (a former plantation between Myrtle Beach and Georgetown, where classical landscaping and outdoor sculpture graced each other): "The Marriage of Society and Christianity."

Yes, a gigantic effigy of Buddha did stand in the county, but as the centerpiece of a miniature golf course.

~~~~

My adjustment to this civilization had already begun, I sometimes remembered, over another silver coffee-service — not of the *James Whitcomb Riley*, but of the parsonage belonging to the First Baptist Church.

On our first visit to Conway, we had been invited there by the Rev. Dr. S. George Lovell. A spiritual oak in the town, Dr. Lovell had a sturdy build, a voice rich and commanding, and a gaze as steady as his jaw — all of this winningly compromised by a lively sense of humor. ("Who does he remind me of?" I kept wondering.) As Mrs. Lovell poured graciously, the two young guests felt special indeed.

Accompanying us — indeed, our key to the house as well as to the town — was the obstetrician who wanted to hire Marge. After geting up at night for decades to deliver babies, Dr. Collins had somehow remained alert and even genial. Now he was tugging and rotating on our behalf, because Dr. Lovell possessed some official and unofficial influence at the college. Late in the summer a teaching job opened up at the Air Force base, and I was invited to fill it. I found myself in the Military-Protestant complex.

The story continues at the First Baptist day-care center. On its floor Andrea took her first step. Soon she was toddling around outside picking up acorns: "Steeple!" she would exclaim, pointing between dark, rambling boughs that looked as if an ocean had withdrawn to leave strands of gray seaweed hung from every twig.

One evening after we waterskied with friends, I waded ashore to spot that gray steeple rising above the trees far up Elm Street. It was always the first thing visible in Conway when we returned over the old causeway. It signified "Almost home"—unlike the steeple in Port Gibson, Mississippi, whose golden hand-and-finger had pointed toward the heavens and signified "Almost to work" (to me, at least).

As a toddler, Andrea would wend her way from the day care to the library. One time I pulled a loose brick off a wall and urged her to do the same with a stuck one. (She neither got the joke nor minded it.) Sometimes we walked along Elm Street, other times Laurel. Perhaps we would stroll downtown past the three Methodist Churches—old, older, and oldest, all in a row. The earliest one bore a sign, "Men's Bible Class, founded 1919." Next to that building rose tombstones dating back to the early 1800s. Shading them was a thick oak whose roots on one side had tilted an obelisk, and on the other had pushed under the brick wall. The tree arched over both graveyard and sidewalk, nearly touching the live oak branches across the street by the post office, covering citizens of nearly two centuries.

Our daughter's baby-sitters took her to evening services at Maple Baptist or the Church of God ("That's OK, I don't take money on Sunday"). After nursery school at the First Methodist Church, Andrea went exploring with her dad and was rewarded with a private concert by the organist. Then at a "living Christmas tree" chorale at the First Baptist Church, she saw Miss Evelyn Snider, the narrator, her hair pulled into a snug bun.

With time my disdain for the notion of adult Sunday School even diminished. Although resenting the way it took up people's social lives, I wondered at the temerity I had shown in questioning this institution. For "My Sunday School class" was a clan. It offered secret pals, gifts, parties, discussions, prayer, music, spiritual retreats. . . . Perhaps I even came to half-like the idea.

Members of the community often seemed genuinely impelled by spiritual forces. Dr. Brake, for example, had spent two weeks in Central America at his own expense assisting a medical mission. Various members of the Lions Club, a den of deacons, touched me with their faith. When my own heritage rose within me like a tide, I wondered whether a purely secular community would seem like home.

Yet when an actor in an amateur play—a courtroom drama performed in the old Mills courthouse itself—refused to swear on the Bible and declared, "It's no use, I'm an atheist," I suddenly felt that windows had been thrown open to a fresh breeze.

As a former Glen Ellynite, I felt grateful for a ceremony in the First Baptist Church. The daughter of one Lion was marrying the son of another Lion—one who owned a lumberyard that deserved a historical marker and submitted to inventory every hundred years. As I listened to the organ echo against the large, austere sanctuary of the First Baptist Church, I found myself carried by memory to the Congregational Church on the corner of Forest and Anthony.

On the outside it was a brick fortress. Rather than a steeple it had a square belfry with spires at each corner. Inside, too, it expressed the stability, restraint, and grandeur that the town valued in its Christianity.

Every month or two, the children would be brought up by a kind of secret passageway to the "Big Church." There, upon red cushions that contrasted with dark wood, we sat hushed, folding no paper airplanes, perhaps just turning around to look at the balcony at the north end or gazing up at the lamps that hung down from the lofty peak. At the south end sat the choir. Divided into two groups that faced each other from the sides, the members were robed and well trained. They sat above and behind a low wooden wall that defined the back of the stagelike area reserved for golden candlesticks, Bible, pulpit, and the minister's chair. The organist, like God himself, was concealed yet shook the place with a rumbling and trumpeting harmony. Then the Rev. Mr. Stevens walked to the pulpit. Tall, wearing a severe black vestment with only a little concession to trimming, he looked like a Protestant pope, or more logically, a Puritan divine without a hat.

Before he could begin his sermon of yesteryear, the bride walked down the aisle on the arm of her Lion father. Soon she would be married and live next door.

~~~

In trying to reach a *modus vivendi*, I was grateful most of all for the Church of St. Leo. This brotherhood had been chartered in Conway forty years earlier.

Almost every Friday afternoon at one o'clock, I would enter a room partitioned off from the rest of Conway Motor Inn. My hand would disappear into the warm grip of the usher, Lion Jack, who asked about my family. Up in front stood the long head table with white altar cloths and, in the middle, a pulpit featuring the profiles of two golden lion heads. A violet liturgical banner with golden symbols sewn upon it hung on the wall behind the President, Secretary, Lion of the Week and his guest. To the left of the head table stood the American flag, and to the right, the South Carolina flag next to the piano.

Lioness Rod (organist and choir director of Kingston Presbyterian Church) provided a lively prelude such as "The Washington and Lee Swing," as if daring age to catch her fingers. Sitting at paper place-mats, the communicants munched a salad before the blessing. As with many churches, a number of members felt the need to sit in the same pew each week. Gong! The bronze bell signaled us to rise for the Pledge of Allegiance, then to sing "My Country 'Tis of Thee," for which I ventured the bass line, then to hear a prayer by this year's Chaplain and to ratify it by a communal "Amen."

Then we break bread together, actually biscuit. The meal comes from a fixed list. Perhaps it is chicken (the "old red rooster" of my exegesis) along with rice and gravy, lima beans, sweetened ice tea, and a ritual food known as "pineapple puddin'." We check the bulletin for the speaker's name and for club news, and we talk about sports, the Conway scene, families, business. As in all churches, one might have nothing in common with a few members except membership itself. I ask one Lion about his daughter, my former student, and someone with a new baby compliments Marge. Asking for the tea pitcher, Lion T.J. laughs about his visiting son-in-law consuming his larder. Someone gets a little free advice about air-conditioning from Lion John. The elderly Judge is shaky of fork but sharp of mind, and when I comment on his long, rich life, he avers, "The Lord's been good to me."

It's time for the collection. The Tail Twister gets the porcelain chamber pot from the head table and walks among the parishioners to see who must pay a dime for being late or wearing unsuitable clothing.

Now the familiar chords resound as we stand to sing "Happy Birthdays" and "Happy Anniversaries." At the Song Leader's behest we open our booklets to the old favorites, "It's a Grand Old Flag" or "Tell Me Why" or "The Lions Roar."

After some comedy by the Tail Twister, guests are introduced, announcements are made, and the speaker is introduced. The sermon is a twenty-minute talk of varying interest. It might cover the Bloodmobile, the bond referendum, the job of a veterinarian, the prospects of the high school football team. . . . A few listeners nod.

Then the President thanks the speaker, invites the guests back, reminds the members about this or that (perhaps about recalling a sick member in their prayers), and whacks the bell with the gavel, sometimes only after the Lion Judge stands up and declares impishly, "Two o'clock, time to go." Whereupon the brethren shake hands and depart—full, edified, ready to go, and glad to belong.

15

Rhythms II

Now when the sun went down—could that be cool air? Even in the daytime a breeze would trespass on the stronghold of summer. An old woman carefully made her way across the street wearing an old-lady dress and a wide-rimmed hat, hugging a mess o' collards. One day we found a pumpkin and some popcorn cobs left on our porch by Farmer Long.

The field had reverted to dirt. Another crop then inched up, rye grass. As it grew, the barns behind seemed to retreat over a hill. Walking along the sandy road I saw the farmer next to a line of cows that bellowed and ambled toward the barn. Then a calf started tipping from forefeet to hindfeet with its back rigid, like a toy rocking-cow. "They've been eating acorns," explained Mr. Long. "They're not hungry —usually they're eager to get into the barn with its food." One gray autumn day, the cows standing against the green-glowing blades of grass made the definitive contrast between animal and vegetable.

In the house, insects had begun to clear out for the winter. Although raised where the exterminator came in an unmarked car, I had settled where the cockroach was the state insect (figuratively speaking). The euphemism "Palmetto bug" gave scant comfort when a person trod barefoot through a dark house. A blow against the roach was a blow for the clean home and the pure. Saint Francis himself would hurl a shoe. Before we finally turned to poison, the roach had appeared on the cover of all our magazines.

A trail of sugar ants would run along the kitchen counters. Poison merely shifted their point of entry, even to the telephone box, so for a time we all shared a link to the outside. Finally we learned to leave not the tiniest vestige of meals. The few lean scouts that returned were dispatched by magic drops.

Broad leaves of tobacco again sailed from under the canopies of trucks and floated to the road for me to show Andrea a leaf. One such vehicle pulled a low trailer with a half-dozen bags on it, fat and sagging, the broad leaves sticking out the top to shine gold and brown in the morning sun. Luckily for my own health I had become somewhat desensitized to the weed's toxicity. For tobacco was in the atmosphere both literally and figuratively.

This was the true Marlboro Country. But instead of stallions, Horry County Cadillacs (pickups); instead of cowboy hats, Caterpillar caps. At summer's end, school began without a few pupils who had to finish cutting the farm leaf before turning the book leaf. One woman told me that her mother (wife of my Kabar acquaintance) used to send her care packages to Clemson wrapped with tobacco twine. Some motels at the beach were built by tobacco money. Even my big secondhand typewriter had been "used only during the tobacco season" (evidently to peck leaves into snuff). Conway Hospital not only permitted cigarettes but sold them.

Time to plant rye grass after September 1. Look out, after a few days it will shoot up. I could not believe this grass that stayed bright green until summer, nor could I understand Mrs. McMillan's aversion: "It doesn't look like winter."

With Labor Day the mass of tourists en route to and from Myrtle Beach had disappeared. No longer did the Lions have to wait for long concatenations of vehicles with different-hued license plates. Just a few cars, motor homes, and campers dribbled past.

Locals had dominion at the beach. Here was the best land in Horry County, even though it lay under water twice a day. From the shore, Dad entered the impertinent, stinging waves using his tiptoe-and-gasp style. Then while Mom negotiated her own entry, Andrea already frolicked in the waves, her laugh no longer showing only two teeth. On the way home the turntable bridge might revolve to let another Northern yacht pass toward Florida.

Autumn brought the scent of flounder at the annual Shriners' Fish Fry. Residents chatted in the cool air while sipping Pepsi or iced tea and flaking luscious meat from delicate bones. I easily overlooked the extra salt, the clamminess of the sweet potatoes, and the plastic ashtrays that advertised Goldfinch Funeral Home. Autumn also summoned boats camouflaged with fronds and pulled along the streets toward one river or another. On Halloween, pickup trucks from out in the countryside unloaded children to forage along the town's streets.

"Want to go to the hoochie-koochie show?" It was Richard Lovelace on the phone. I always admired his ability as a settler to be involved and yet detached. He could nurture a growing law practice, engage in public service, socialize with the prominent, love the area, and relish its excesses. Soon we headed northward with a driver who toted a large bourbon and water.

The fair itself resembled one that came to Glen Ellyn each year except for that extra attraction—"It's showtime, Go time!"—whose mysteries I dared not reveal and whose existence in the Bible Belt I could not explain.

Robins, on their way farther south, dropped by to peck the yard. Snakes looked for a winter home, caterpillars stuffed themselves, geese honked to clear the right-of-way. Although foliage still abounded, it slowed, except for the red tips of maples. Dogwoods drained all their blood to the leaves; then they dropped berries so glossy and red that I seemed to shrink closer to the sidewalk, like a small boy again—perhaps on a Sunday School outing, as we shuffled through oak leaves on Ellyn Place and turned up cocoons, symbols of life in death.

In late November, during the Clemson-Carolina football game, the Wells family gaily cycled through a town empty of all but children and squirrels.

~~~

The crèche appeared again in front of the courthouse. Near it, strings of colored lights covered a great, full tree, which in the daytime was clearly a magnolia. On a yard near town, one of the plaster Magi would tire of his vigil by the stable and lie down for several days at a time. Many citizens put up trees at the beginning of December, perhaps to compensate for the lack of bracing weather. One day we drove to a Christmas-tree farm next to a building studded with hubcaps; although enjoying the excursion and admiring our fresh-cut tree, we felt ambivalent about the uncanonical cedar with its sharp prickles. And I tried to ignore our new ornament, an oyster shell with a Christmas tree painted on it.

In the Lions Club, this season brought the annual concert by Lioness Rod's children's choir. They proceeded through the congregation of St. Leo and stood there looking shy, mischievous, and taller than last year. And one night Marge and I were surprised by a pickup load of carolers made up of young acquaintances from the swimming pool.

I worked the Salvation Army kettle with Lion Rick McIver, the lumberyard owner, whose suspenders were concealed by a red plaid jacket. An authority on local history, he explained that a black student of mine, who had just made a contribution, had descended from a Polish slave owner. In Rick's slightly low-country accent I heard a faint echo of the ancient black dialect that had influenced white speech along the coast. Indeed, older blacks and whites had an exotic way of pronouncing the town's name as "Cahwn-vay."

Happy to be invited to another Couples Club dance at the National Guard Armory, we mingled with young and old, sometimes with parents and their grown children. Although the building was more capacious than elegant, we felt gratified to know so many people as everyone sipped drinks by the lights of a two-story-high Christmas tree, ate fancy hors d'oeuvres, and danced as the band played such ritual songs as "I Love Beach Music." The step of choice was called the Shag. Although *it* varied a bit from the jitterbug of Fortnight Club, I was unable to.

On New Year's Day we had tasted a good-luck dish of dried peas cooked in a pork broth. "For real Hoppin' John," my informant confided, "you gotta have a piece o' hog jowl."

Patches of collards, those thick-leaved, homely-headed wonders, defied the cold. For the fireplace I cut up the last of our pine, using a railroad tie as a chopping block. Although by now I could see that pine burned up more quickly than hardwood, I still could not disparage it like a native. Rather, I admired those orange flames that had, ultimately, come from a cone. On the farm, viewed from the highway, a patch of leafless hardwoods in the pines seemed like a wisp of pale smoke rising from one of the barns. On

Lakeland Avenue, the shafts from the evening sun made the leaves of a bush glow in the cold—and among them, could those be pink petals? Camellias! In the South, Old Man Winter sported a boutonniere.

Children at day-care centers were kept inside when the temperature dropped to Invigorating. The North, however, did stray as far as South Carolina one day: snow fell and stuck, so that Marge and I excitedly pulled Andrea around town with a rope attached to a galvanized tub. Then the regular cold weather resumed: gloves on in the morning, off in the afternoon. At the beach, commercial areas had a Wednesday-afternoon-in-Glen-Ellyn look.

Around Valentine's Day the Lions held the annual Ladies Night. Sad to say, the group of widows in red dresses was newly augmented this year by the wife of Lion Skeets Solomon.

The private academy once again held its pork barbecue fundraiser on a Friday in Lent. Our fragrant jessamine vine bloomed again on a tree beside the driveway, and I halfway understood what my eyes had been trying to tell me, that the live oaks were shedding old leaves for new. Pine pollen covered everything just in time for the Lions broom sale. This year Andrea went around with me for a while, carrying a red handled, child-sized broom that would never brush snow from leggings. Among my customers was a couple who declared that they had planted every tree on the property thirty years before; they had never trimmed their big dogwood but instead made their grumbling friends detour off the walk and around its limbs.

One old lady explained her refusal to buy a broom by derogating her previous purchase: "Hit was so stubborn until I quit using it." Some people down the street composed a scene of such utter relaxation, both physical and cultural, that I almost gave them a broom. Framed between a jacked-up car and its open hood, they lounged on the front porch, whose half-bricked pillars sagged at the middle. While the couple leaned on the sofa, a woman smoked on the steps; at her waist an inch of pantyhose showed above her ample spandex britches, with a patch of skin over that.

On the farm, with the tractor in profile way back in the field, the driver wearing a pith helmet and leaning over the steering wheel — all resembled a still photograph except for the big grids that slowly rotated with the tire. Sometimes a cloud of dust betrayed motion, sometimes black mud turning to brown dirt behind a plow. One morning a flock of birds pecked at the dirt when suddenly gray wings beat upward against gray water pellets. After a few mornings the dirt had grown a stubble of green. The crop then rose until it eventually obscured the far woods from the road.

Near the Conway bus station, across from a triangle made by highways 501, 378, and 701, the drone of beach traffic was muted by trees and grass, by rows of leafy, ground-hugging vegetables, and by a patch of tall plants. Bamboo? Not skinny enough. It was sugar cane. The thin leaves curved downward from far over the two gardeners, billowing and glowing under the gray sky. Part of this jungle already lay horizontal with its thin blades tangled. Nearby extended a pile of long, naked, segmented poles that resembled fat cornstalks or slightly purple bones, but with hairy roots. A lot of tooth exercise to come. The silver machete seemed incongruous in the hands of the unprepossessing woman as she hacked and tossed. Occasionally she spoke to her companion, whose suspenders were half-hidden in the stalks; a slight lilt in her voice suggested the Caribbean and before that West Africa. Her black skin — did it give off magical tints?

~~~~

The Season was once again upon the area. Locals took special care when driving on Friday evenings, Saturday mornings (checkout time for weekly rentals), and Sundays. The Chinese man drew stares with the candle in his head (an effigy at Ripley's), an obese woman at a campground sat sideways in a car while a boy shaved her legs, radio stations advised sunbathers to "Turn or you'll burn," and at night, vehicles slowly cruised Ocean Boulevard, many of them four-wheeled radios, while families played miniature golf around plastic cornstalks and gigantic pandas with blinking red eyes.

It was hard to believe that the 1841 map of South Carolina I had bought showed not one settlement along the coast of Horry County. In fact, although a few roads appeared, Conwayboro was the only town named. It marked the center of a pale pink, diamond-shaped blank that extended between several swashes to the east and, to the west, several ferries, one of them "Potatobed," where my canoeing party had stopped for lunch.

Spending the night at the beach on July Fourth, Marge and I strolled over to the ocean and down the strand. BANG! POP! At every step a firecracker went off on the beach. A little rocket whizzed past us to extinguish itself in the water. Like Francis Scott Key, we watched the explosions and the cascades of silver, scarlet, and electric emerald that illuminated the pier, beach houses, white surf, and crowds. Laughing and holding tight to each other, we retreated from the battlefield.

All summer long in Conway, peaches were trucked in from the Sand Hills region and sold from a shaded tailgate on Main Street. Birds again made a home and privy of our fireplace, so I had to call the Clemson Extension agent to

learn how to evict them. Sometimes, for the neighborhood kids, I took a chunk of coquina and drew hopscotch squares on the new asphalt surface of Graham Road.

Around the first of August, onlookers walked next to rusty tin siding, past the Tobacco Queen and congressman, past the old man peddling watermelon from his truck, to enter the Horry Warehouse downtown. Piles of tobacco leaves bulged upon burlap bags set in rows, and the aroma invited a nonsmoker to reconsider. There was the Extension agent speaking on TV. The auctioneer began striding up and down the rows, holding a cigarette and uttering numbers staccato-style. The buyers in tow behind him responded with loud "Yeahs" or grunts. He scrutinized their hands, which flashed one or more finger-cents. Dark-tanned farmers, a few of them blacks, watched from beneath caps. Overhead a sign proclaimed, "Fine tobaccos for Marlboro, Parliament and Philip Morris Purchased at This Market." I wondered how much of Horry County had made its way to my hometown.

As someone paid mainly by tax money, and fond of numerous students who had worked 'bacca, I even found myself hoping that this year's price was decent.

In September I decided not to plant rye grass because it extended summer into what little winter there was.

16

Tick-Tock Town

The A&P now opened on Sunday. It forced me to anguish over whether or not to buy some potatoes on the Sabbath and jeopardize a long-standing habit. Coors Beer was now sold in the Independent Republic, rather than confined to an alpine region where my cooling six-pack once floated away in the rapids. And when I finally asked for a glass of iced tea, my hostess had none.

"What? Every Southern house has iced tea in the refrigerator."

"We don't keep that stuff anymore—it's got caffeine." She poured me a sugar-free lemonade.

By the time the chickens had quit strutting near the Conway National Bank, its radio advertisements sounded blandly national—despite phrases like "right here in Horry County."

I found myself comparing how another place had become less of a tight village over the years.

The last wartime chicken in Glen Ellyn left the garage for the plate, and the coops on the perimeter of town emptied and began to rot. The last piece of coal for the snowman's eyes disappeared, as did the frozen columns of cream that pushed up the necks and through the tops of milk bottles on the back porch, as did the milkman himself, following the iceman who had wielded his great tongs down at "Grandma" Allen's. In the Raffenspargers' yard, the new residents continued to dump compost and refuse into the mysterious indentation that marked an old well, until at last it would accept no more. Old Mrs. Clark was taxed out of town.

Every Saturday in summer I awoke to the pounding of hammers, leaf-softened and echoing, as carpenters built houses. Impey's Prairie, where apple trees unaccountably had stood, half-hidden by tall weeds; where children had tunneled their own lovely, dark grave that smelled richly of Mother Earth, only to resurrect themselves into the summer light; where a maple sapling had found itself dug out by father and sons and hauled to a new home on the parkway; where a rivulet had bent the grass southward after a rain; this field was replaced by substantial houses and well-kept lawns. Mrs. Kramer's smoky Indian camp and even Mrs. Clark's house would be sacrificed to a residential cul-de-sac.

A trilevel house arose where my father had showed me how to cover those magic kernels with little mounds of dirt. All around town, sumac, wild asparagus, ragweed, brush, and patches of violets gave way to houses. Even side yards disappeared under foundations. Likewise the fields bordering town. The Munsons built a handsome, ranch-style place at the end of Hawthorn, and not long afterward they could look out the window at a new junior high school, which filled in the places where children had caught tadpoles. At the other end of Kenilworth swamp, a rather severely modern house took shape from the blueprints on the Roses' dining room table. One Thanksgiving or Easter, Cousin Joan and I explored the foundation of a publishing complex that trespassed upon the no man's land next to the Ice Plant, between Glen Ellyn and Wheaton.

Between 1945 and 1960, when I left for college, the population doubled to sixteen thousand.

Sledding grew chancier as traffic increased. "It's getting so crowded," complained Mrs. Kranz, "that I have to drive through the whole downtown in second gear!" One-way streets ran through the business section. Shopping "centers" sprang up outside the village limits. On Roosevelt Road, the Lighthouse Restaurant, with its rather shabby landmark of a tower, vanished. A half-mile away appeared a combination food stand and restaurant; drivers could rush past its rounded-M sign with a bag of ready-made hamburgers. One indication of disappearing farmland: the Chicago radio station that my buddy and I listened to in that pickup, WLS, had just changed its format from pork bellies to pop songs.

~~~~

Conway, we all began to realize, was becoming less of a farming center and more of a bedroom for the beach. Sears & Roebuck abandoned its catalogue outlet on Fourth Avenue and opened a large retail store in the new Myrtle Square Mall. A proliferation of condos helped extend "the Season," a term that had once been agricultural. So Labor Day no longer turned Highway 501 into a bare road: out-of-state cars and motor homes, even tour buses with alien names like "Dominico," began to compete with commuter vehicles, including the vans that carried black women to clean motel rooms.

I now viewed the Bypass as a sort of Charlotte and North Western Railway. Not a bypass at all, it split the town in two. Along its four lanes sped thousands of commuters between Conway and the beach. Hundreds of thousands of impatient tourists looked out the window to know Conway only as a strip of restaurants and several frustrating traffic lights. The same highways that had made Conway a center were now making it a bottleneck.

One more indignity. "Waccamaw"—the name for that tannic pathway of the Indian canoe, for that road of the raft, the oar-propelled boat, the current-powered barge, the sidewheeler churning its way up the slippery black incline, the tugboat throbbing low in the night, and the nearly airborne Mercury outboard—had begun to serve as the colloquial abbreviation for "Waccamaw Pottery," a warehouse complex on Highway 501 across from Waccamaw Brick that sold indigenous items like cement pelicans and Philippine baskets.

In the neighborhood the SCREE and CHUFF of the sawmill had been suburb-muffled. Among our neighbors, transience was the rule. One by one, people built new houses and then sold them when opportunity or divorce knocked at the door. Only the sprinkling of original houses kept their owners.

The college, in its beginning a self-help effort like the telephone cooperative, had started off in Conway High School only twenty years earlier. Local students still tended to be homebodies, but they were more likely to meet out-of-staters. One local might ask another, "Do you stay nearer Galivants Ferry or Centenary?" But the day was coming when a Philadelphian would jokingly ask a New Jerseyite, "Which exit do *you* live on?" I was less likely to read an essay about working tobacco (about getting dirt and gum on one's clothes, picking up leaves with toes when the boss was gone, getting caught breaking a leaf) and more likely to read about driving a bread truck at the beach, working a motel desk, waiting on tables, or maintaining a golf course, where the balls scattered on the practice range resembled constellations. Adding to the variety, a few more of the local students were black. At least one started her day by boating across the Waccamaw from an island community near Brookgreen Gardens. Conway got its first Jacuzzi. When the first BMW automobile whirred down the street, I was a little apprehensive lest it run over Tom Thumb—especially after learning that the pianist for that ceremony was none other than Lioness Rod.

In town the chicken-washing gas station had been replaced by a store advertising a continual New Crop Pecans. The Conway Stock Yards had disappeared. So had the *Samson II* tugboat, because the river mill now transported logs solely by truck. Even the Horry Drug Store existed only in the scrapbook of memory—Freshidor, Frisbee, and all.

"Folks," commented one old-timer, "just don't go to church on Wednesday night like they used to." Doubts nagged me, too, about the increasing homogenization of the area. I recalled my brother's satisfaction when an interstate highway designed to reach his isolated town in West Virginia was not funded: "I want people to *earn* their way here." Just as I had become a Nothiner—no longer Northern yet not Southern—Conway was becoming more like Anywhere, U.S.A. I felt ambivalent about furthering the process. Marge and I had not only replaced a bit of wilderness with our new house but had given little reinforcement to native customs. Even the college (where I now worked full time) was an agent of change. Just as the dome of its outdoor columned atheneum was not congruent with a church steeple, its values had a problematical relationship with those of religion.

The change was continuing with our daughter, who, for example, liked peanuts "balled" but called them "boiled." She tripped around the house singing "Kids in Chicago / Havin' a good time, / They're all watchin' / Channel Nine" after the television cable began importing WGN.

That spring day on the trestle when I searched the Waccamaw River for a sign: had I been looking at the wrong thing? Perhaps I should have focused on the bridges. The Old Highway 501 bridge over the river, even the railroad trestle—these had been augurs of the future. As a newcomer struck with the town's rural heritage, had I not underestimated the impact of the highways? They had been carrying changes for the past three-quarters of a century, making the Republic less and less independent.

~~~

In the Red & White grocery store, before it burned down, I enjoyed a cordial encounter with the Rev. Dr. George Lovell. Turning away I beheld as if in a vision the person he resembled: the late Fred L. Biester, principal or superintendent for forty-four years.

Perhaps it was fitting, I conceded little by little, that a clock should mark the most prominent corner of both Conway and Glen Ellyn. For is not a place a time? Is not a town a transition? Home-time, tick-tock-town. "We crossed the tracks," wrote Tom's sister about a visit to the suburb of her youth, "noticing, remembering, disapproving, sometimes making concessions and approving of a change. Mostly we approved of the things that had remained the same." The years, like the asphalt surface that now covered Graham Road and had already covered the tar-mended streets of Glen Ellyn, do bring good, bad, and indifferent changes that obscure the past to all but memory.

Driving from Conway toward the North Carolina–Atlantic Ocean corner of Horry County, you might make a left turn off Highway 90, travel for a bucolic mile, then make another left onto a dirt road. It has been scraped between fields of the same tan color. Shortly beyond a tobacco barn, it passes beneath the arch of an oak bough and into the Tilly Swamp community, a settlement populated mainly by relatives, some buried in its graveyard. The first dwelling is voluminous, as much porch as house, with a washing machine squatting metallically between the back railing and the horizontal white boards of the exterior. From the dust of the driveway rises an antique gasoline pump once used for farm equipment. Next door, beyond the *pee*kan trees, is a smallish brick house. You are in Old Horry County, where children and grandchildren stay next to Grandma. Beg pardon: Great Grandma.

But next to the coon-dog cage, a white dish-antenna tips toward the sky. In the driveway is a Mercedes Benz station wagon that Daddy uses in his job as a mechanic for an automobile dealership on Highway 501 between Conway and Myrtle Beach. His grandfather had been a farmer and had also operated Reaves Ferry across the Waccamaw a few hundred feet away. Mama works at the Beach for AVX, a company that makes electronic capacitors. Their daughter will do well in college.

Time once sent a plague of beetles to Glen Ellyn. Mr. Kranz was able to hire a truck with a winch that put in a half-grown elm to replace his dead one; but most of the residents had to be content with elm stumps and maple saplings. Gone were the arches beneath which Mrs. Groom's second graders sang "Here comes the groom, / Skinny as a broom" as they promenaded to the public library.

Yet also with time came a new community college on the outskirts of town. It grew quickly and enjoyed local admiration. And as the years passed, judging from the names in the telephone book, many descendents of Eastern European emigrants were able to move to Glen Ellyn from the city.

As a sort of immigrant to Conway, I found myself grateful that a place itself does not "stay." Nor is it, I mused, an original, ideal entity that gets corrupted by the calendar.

We slow the passage of years with our heirlooms and land-marks, with our rituals and rhythms, even with our com-memorative books. But time, like an ever-flowing stream, bears all its towns away.

Again that impulse seized me to jump into the river and go swimming! And so I did.